AIR FORCE FELLOWS

COLLEGE OF AEROSPACE DOCTRINE, RESEARCH AND EDUCATION

AIR UNIVERSITY

The Future of NATO-Russian Relations
or *How to Dance with a Bear and Not Get Mauled*

GORDON B. HENDRICKSON
Lieutenant Colonel, USAF

Walker Paper No. 6

Air University Press
Maxwell Air Force Base, Alabama 36112-6615

July 2006

Air University Library Cataloging Data

Hendrickson, Gordon B.
    The future of NATO-Russian relations, or How to dance with a bear and not get mauled / Gordon B. Hendrickson.
       p. ; cm. – (Walker paper, 1555-7871 ; no. 6)
    Includes bibliographical references.

    1. North Atlantic Treaty Organization—Russia (Federation). 2. Russia (Federation)—Foreign relations. 3. North Atlantic Treaty Organization—Membership. I. Title. II. Series.

    355.031091821—dc22

This Walker Paper and others in the series are available electronically at the Air University Research Web site http://research.maxwell.af.mil and the AU Press Web site http://aupress.maxwell.af.mil.

Air Force Fellows

Since 1958 the Air Force has assigned a small number of carefully chosen, experienced officers to serve one-year tours at distinguished civilian institutions studying national security policy and strategy. Beginning with the 1994 academic year, these programs were accorded in-residence credit as part of professional military education at senior service schools. In 2003 these fellowships assumed senior developmental education (SDE) force-development credit for eligible officers.

The SDE-level Air Force Fellows serve as visiting military ambassadors to their centers, devoting effort to expanding their colleagues' understanding of defense matters. As such, candidates for SDE-level fellowships have a broad knowledge of key Department of Defense (DOD) and Air Force issues. SDE-level fellows perform outreach by their presence and voice in sponsoring institutions. They are expected to provide advice as well as promote and explain Air Force and DOD policies, programs, and military-doctrine strategy to nationally recognized scholars, foreign dignitaries, and leading policy analysts. The Air Force Fellows also gain valuable perspectives from the exchange of ideas with these civilian leaders. SDE-level fellows are expected to apprise appropriate Air Force agencies of significant developments and emerging views on defense as well as economic and foreign policy issues within their centers. Each fellow is expected to use the unique access she or he has as grounds for research and writing on important national security issues. The SDE Air Force Fellows include the National Defense Fellows, the RAND Fellows, the National Security Fellows, and the Secretary of Defense Corporate Fellows. In addition, the Air Force Fellows program supports a post-SDE military fellow at the Council on Foreign Relations.

On the level of intermediate developmental education, the chief of staff approved several Air Force Fellowships focused on career broadening for Air Force majors. The Air Force Legislative Fellows program was established in April 1995, with the Foreign Policy Fellowship and Defense Advanced Research Projects Agency Fellowship coming under the Air Force Fellows program in 2003. In 2004 the Air Force Fellows also assumed responsibility for the National Laboratories Technologies Fellows.

Contents

Illustration

Foreword

Throughout the Cold War, the NATO allies and the Soviet Union faced each other as adversaries, constantly preparing for and investing enormous resources against the real possibility of a major armed conflict in Europe and the North Atlantic region. Thankfully, the end of the Cold War changed all that. After the fall of the Berlin Wall and subsequent collapse of the Soviet Union almost 15 years ago, NATO subsequently opened its doors to any member of the former Soviet Union and Warsaw Pact willing to join the alliance and able to meet its entry criteria. Since that time, 10 countries—all former Soviet satellites—have joined NATO's ranks through two rounds of expansion. During this time, and despite palpable Russian discomfort with the prospect of the alliance drawing ever closer to its borders, NATO-Russian relations have been marked by unprecedented and increasing cooperation in a number of different fields and venues.

There is, however, a good chance the alliance may undertake yet another round of expansion in the future, to include the possibility of offering membership to countries that share significant borders as well as long-standing historic and cultural ties with Russia. In addition, an increasingly self-confident Russia is now attempting to exert greater political and economic influence in the Eurasian region and to once again be seen as a world power. How can NATO effectively deal with these dynamics and continue to work cooperatively with Russia?

In this paper, Lt Col Gordy Hendrickson offers some answers. He examines the recent history of the relationship and the Russian perspectives on that history and addresses many of the potentially contentious issues still facing NATO and Russia. He then outlines a useful framework for interaction between the two sides—a framework which can form the foundation for concrete actions and programs to continue down the path of mutual cooperation. Colonel Hendrickson concludes by proposing several practical steps the alliance can take to continue to effectively work with Russia and keep the relationship moving forward.

It is absolutely vital that NATO and Russia get this right. Despite areas of potential disagreement, there is still much room for cooperation between the two parties. However, they must both seek to avoid old patterns of distrust and zero-sum competition—certainly a task easier said than done. But with a joint commitment to cooperation in working through the inevitable challenges, NATO and Russia can, and must, navigate the path ahead together. This thought-provoking and timely paper offers valuable insight into how to do just that.

FRANK G. KLOTZ
Lieutenant General, USAF

About the Author

Lt Col Gordon B. Hendrickson

Lt Col Gordon B. Hendrickson currently serves as Special Advisor to the Vice President for National Security Affairs, where he provides recommendations and guidance on a broad range of European and Eurasian matters. He is experienced in every intelligence discipline across a wide variety of duties at the national, theater, and unit levels.

Colonel Hendrickson was commissioned with military distinction in 1985 from the US Air Force Academy, Colorado Springs, Colorado, where he earned a bachelor of science degree in Russian history. He also holds a master of arts degree in international relations from Creighton University, Omaha, Nebraska; a master of arts degree in national security affairs, Soviet/East European Studies, from the Naval Postgraduate School, Monterey, California; and a master of military operational art and science degree from the Air Command and Staff College, Maxwell AFB, Alabama.

Colonel Hendrickson's career includes duties as an intelligence analyst, weaponeer and target developer, command briefer, foreign area officer, telecommunications and computer security chief, and wing executive officer. He served a joint tour as assistant air attaché and air attaché to the US Embassy in Moscow, Russia, and commanded the 381st Intelligence Squadron at Elmendorf AFB, Alaska. Most recently, he was a Senior Fellow at the Atlantic Council of the United States in Washington, DC. His personal awards include the Defense

Meritorious Service Medal, Meritorious Service Medal with three oak leaf clusters, Air Force Commendation Medal with oak leaf cluster, and Air Force Achievement Medal.

Preface

The genesis of this paper began several years ago while I was living in Europe and NATO began considering its most recent rounds of enlargement. During four years of extensive travel throughout Western Europe and two years of working in the US Embassy in Moscow, I could clearly see the impact that relations between NATO and the Russian Federation have, not only on their foreign and defense policies, but also the very real and personal impact they have on me as a US military officer. As a result, when the opportunity for additional research arose, I wanted to understand better the issues and stakes involved in such an important relationship.

I found most of my material for this project from local sources in the Washington, DC, area; from NATO printed publications and materials; and from Internet sources. I used materials from all sides of the problem and from all significant parties involved.

I would like to gratefully acknowledge the assistance of my Senior Fellowship institution, the Atlantic Council of the United States (ACUS). Lyn Soudien and Matt Schumann were terrific in helping to facilitate what was a rich and rewarding year of "broadening my horizons." I also thank Fran Burwell and Sara Tesorieri for the opportunity to see and experience Europe's leadership institutions firsthand, as well as my colleagues and other Senior Fellows at ACUS for their comments and discussions during the writing and presentation of this paper. Their perspectives and insights helped me to understand better the wide range of views represented in this important area and to form my own views on this relationship. Finally and most importantly, I thank my wife, Kim, for her patience and support during my seemingly endless research, and for once again tolerating the stacks of source materials that invaded our home these past months.

GORDON B. HENDRICKSON
Lieutenant Colonel, USAF

Abstract

Since the dissolution of the Soviet Union and the Warsaw Pact, NATO has enlarged its membership twice with countries formerly under Soviet influence and control and, as of this writing, is preparing to begin the process for a third expansion. Russia has watched the borders of NATO creep ever closer to its own but has generally been powerless to prevent it. Although NATO has taken pains to include and consult with Russia regarding its actions and future plans, former air attaché to the US Embassy in Moscow Gordon Hendrickson contends the Kremlin cannot reasonably be expected to continue to watch NATO's eastward expansion without eventually pushing back hard. Without question, many significant issues and challenges must still be solved before enlarging the alliance once again. In light of this, the author says NATO must work rigorously to continue to keep Russia engaged in a productive and mutually beneficial relationship as both sides work through the future obstacles that inevitably will arise in the NATO-Russian relationship.

Although the relationship is continuing to evolve, Hendrickson's research led him to the conclusion that, in order to keep Russia reassured and working productively with NATO, there are a number of concrete actions the alliance can and must take to avoid squandering the historic opportunity before it.

Chapter 1

Introduction

We need to be Russia's toughest critic, but we also need to be Russia's best friend.

—Cong. Curt Weldon

Over the past decade, the North Atlantic Treaty Organization (NATO) has undergone the most significant changes of its more than 50-year life. Since the end of the Cold War, NATO has expanded twice, in 1999 and 2004, and has added 10 new members in the past six years. The alliance has also undergone a fundamental shift in focus, from a purely collective defense alliance designed to counter the Soviet and Warsaw Pact threat during the Cold War to a collective security organization designed to bolster and fortify the overall security posture of the Euro-Atlantic area. This shift has also significantly included a new NATO mission of out-of-area operations, most notably in Afghanistan and Iraq.

NATO leaders continue to stress that the "door remains open" to even more new members, provided they are willing and able to meet NATO's entrance requirements. As NATO prepares for another likely round of enlargement within the next few years, its leaders must seriously consider the impact yet another growth eastward will have on the Russian Federation. Moscow has thus far accepted with relatively little protest NATO's last two expansion rounds, which encompassed countries formerly under Soviet influence. This was partly due to Russia's inability to effectively prevent the alliance from expanding, as well as the effort alliance leaders made to keep Russia engaged with and included in NATO affairs. However, in considering another round of new members, which undoubtedly will include countries directly bordering the Russian Federation, NATO leaders will have to redouble their efforts and creativity to allay Russian fears of Western encirclement or encroachment. This paper looks at several concrete actions the alliance can take in an effort to reach that goal.

Chapters 2 and 3 provide a history and overview of the development of NATO-Russian relations over the past 15 years since the dissolution of the Soviet Union, along with a survey of Russian attitudes and responses. Chapter 4 examines some of the major contentious issues now facing the two sides, with a particular focus on the underlying sources of those problems that will continue to affect future NATO-Russian dealings. Chapter 5 focuses on many of the cooperative programs and successes the alliance and Russia have achieved in the past few years, and chapter 6 deals with the previously mentioned sources of conflict between NATO and Russia and then outlines several concrete actions NATO can take to continue engaging Russia productively and positively, even in light of another probable round of enlargement.

The NATO-Russian relationship is without question one of the most important and pressing issues that affects overall Euro-Atlantic security. It is a relationship that can, and must, survive future tests of differences in policies, actions, and even sometimes values. However, it is a relationship worth fighting for, and leaders from both sides must find a way to work constructively through their differences. The future of Euro-Atlantic security depends on it.

Chapter 2

Background—The Long Road to Rome

We have come a long way from opposition to dialogue, and from confrontation to cooperation.

—Russian president Vladimir Putin

The Early Years

The relationship between NATO and Russia began informally in December 1991 with the inaugural session of the North Atlantic Cooperation Council (NACC), later renamed the Euro-Atlantic Partnership Council (EAPC). NATO leaders created the council after the end of the Cold War as a forum for political dialogue, consultation, and cooperation in an attempt to foster a new relationship with Central and Eastern European countries.[1] Although it stopped short of establishing a formal relationship between NATO and Russia, it did at least create the initial conditions for the two to begin consultations and dialogue and set the stage for future developments. This was particularly important due to the rapid pace of political change in Europe. In fact, while the NACC was meeting at NATO headquarters for this inaugural session, the Soviet Union actually disintegrated. As a result, the Soviet ambassador present was only able to speak on behalf of the Russian Federation by the time the meeting ended.[2]

The relationship continued after the creation of the EAPC when US president Bill Clinton introduced the Partnership for Peace (PfP), an initiative to reach out to the countries of the former Soviet Union and Warsaw Pact, along with others that also had been under Soviet influence. The PfP was designed to be a major program of practical security and defense cooperation between NATO and individual partner countries and was created to be the operational wing of the EAPC. In particular, the PfP focused, and still does, on activities to help partners build forces capable of participating in peacekeeping operations alongside NATO troops.[3]

By 1994 Russia decided to join the PfP and gradually began to join in a greater degree of cooperation and participation with NATO activities.[4] In 1996 Russian peacekeepers even deployed to Bosnia and Herzegovina to serve alongside their allied counterparts in the NATO-led Implementation Force (IFOR) and later in the Stabilization Force (SFOR) to oversee implementation of the Dayton Peace Accord ending the war in Bosnia and Herzegovina. Notably, the Russian contribution was the largest non-NATO contingent in these forces.[5] Although politically contentious issues surrounding this deployment arose in later months, especially by the end of the 1990s, the fact that Russian forces deployed at all and had regular interaction with NATO forces was significant in itself.

The Founding Act and Permanent Joint Council

President Clinton made the initial decision in the fall of 1996 to push for expansion of NATO's membership ranks. NATO's leaders eventually endorsed Clinton's proposal at the Madrid Summit in July 1997, and NATO subsequently invited Poland, the Czech Republic, and Hungary to start accession talks. In March 1999, these three countries were admitted into the alliance on the eve of its 50th anniversary celebration.[6] The allies also made clear to all that the door was open for the eventual admission of other candidates, according to Article 10 of the Washington Treaty. At the 50th anniversary summit, the alliance specified in its Strategic Concept that "no European democratic country whose admission would fulfill the objectives of the Treaty will be excluded from consideration."[7]

NATO leaders realized that this particular round of expansion—the alliance's fourth since its inception in 1949 but the first after the end of the Cold War—would be particularly sensitive since it would bring former Soviet satellites into the Western alliance. Knowing Russia's perception of NATO as a military bloc hostile to its interests, this was a key issue throughout deliberations for this enlargement. However, Russia had to respect the right of each independent European state to seek its own security arrangements and to belong to international organizations, as well as the right of the members of the alliance to make their own decisions.[8] Although alliance leaders invited several former Warsaw Pact members to join NATO, they also decided a more formal structure should be developed in NATO's relationship with Russia. Their answer was to create a permanent joint council (PJC) for NATO and Russia, giving Russia the capability to sit at the same table with the members of the alliance.

The original purpose of the PJC was to demonstrate in a real and tangible way the shared resolve of NATO member states and Russia to work together more closely towards the common goal of building a lasting and inclusive peace in the Euro-Atlantic area.[9] Thus, formal relations between NATO and Russia began with the signing of the NATO-Russia Founding Act on Mutual Relations, Cooperation, and Security in May 1997. The 1999 50th Anniversary Summit reiterated this important relationship by declaring that "a strong, stable and enduring partnership between NATO and Russia is essential to achieve lasting stability in the Euro-Atlantic area."[10]

With the Founding Act, regular consultations between NATO and Russia began to take place on common security issues. Moscow followed by establishing a Russian mission to NATO, although its personnel were simply taken from, and remained primarily accredited to, Russia's diplomatic mission to Brussels. Under the PJC, the 16 (later 19) NATO allies and Russia sat at the table in a basically consultative format of "16 + 1" (later "19 + 1"). However, one of the biggest drawbacks to this arrangement was that the allies would meet separately beforehand to coordinate all positions on the issues facing the council and then sit down together across from their Russian counterparts with a unified front. Needless to say, open and transparent discussion was not one of the hallmarks of this arrangement.

Although the Founding Act took a good additional step forward in NATO-Russian relations, it unfortunately did not fully close the still-yawning gap between the alliance and Russia. As the ensuing years would reveal, the deep mistrust of the Cold War years proved difficult to overcome, and each side's suspicions of each other's motives persisted. Amb. Nicholas Burns, former US permanent representative to NATO, explained that "one abiding legacy of the Cold War has been a deeply entrenched suspicion of NATO's intentions, especially as the alliance has expanded eastward and struggled to redefine its mission in the post-Soviet world. This feeling of distrust might be best summed up by the idea that, if it is good for NATO, it must be bad for Russia."[11]

As NATO carried out its expansion efforts, coinciding with the European Union's separate efforts to enlarge, Russia remained mostly on the outside. The Kremlin was very much struggling with its own democratic reforms, looking toward the West with both Euro-Atlantic aspirations and some lingering imperial ambitions and wondering where its new place was in the world. Despite increased cooperation through growing shared interests, such as the previously mentioned joint deployment to the Balkans, NATO and Russia still had trouble overcoming the long legacy of Cold War hostility and suspicion.[12] Furthermore, and unfortunately for NATO-Russian relations, the accession of three former Soviet satellites to NATO on the eve of its 50th anniversary also coincided with the eve of the conflict in Kosovo. By this time, rivalry and mutual suspicion had overtly crept into the relationship, culminating in a rupture in relations during the early 1999 Kosovo crisis and Russia's withdrawal from the PJC. According to Paul Fritch, head of the Russia and Ukraine relations section in NATO's Political Affairs and Security Policy Division, when Russia walked out of the PJC, "many on both sides honestly believed that nothing of great value had been lost."[13]

Rome and the NATO-Russia Council

Toward the end of 1999, however, hope once again started to creep back into NATO-Russian relations. When Lord Robertson became NATO secretary general in October of that year, he committed himself to break the stalemate that followed the Kosovo rupture in the relationship. Furthermore, Vladimir Putin announced, following his election as president of Russia in the spring of 2000, that he would work to rebuild relations with NATO in a spirit of pragmatism.[14]

Then came the terrorist attacks of 11 September 2001 and the first-ever invocation of Article 5 of the Washington Treaty.[15] The security challenges now facing the alliance—terrorism, weapons of mass destruction proliferation, regional instability, and trafficking in drugs, arms, and even human beings—clearly showed the West that any lasting solution to these problems would have to include Russia. What was lacking in the PJC, as former NATO secretary general Lord Robertson described it, was "a true sense of shared purpose and urgency." However, the events of 9/11 provided that impetus—"a stark reminder of the need for comprehensive and coordinated action to respond to common threats."[16]

As a result NATO leaders decided a new forum was necessary. After discussions at the Rome Summit in May 2002, they agreed that, despite a joint commitment to peacekeeping in the Balkans and the development of a substantial program of practical security and defense-related cooperation, underlying "inhibitions" remained on both sides and should be dealt with in a new organization. The May 2002 Rome Declaration on "NATO-Russia Relations: A New Quality" thus established the NATO-Russia Council (NRC), which met for the first time in May 2003 in Moscow.

The timing of the NRC's establishment was none too soon, as it coincided with several other significant events in US, European, and Russian relations, including welcoming seven new members into the alliance in 2004 and creating a partnership with the European Union (EU) under Berlin Plus.[17] The NRC reinforced the need for coordinated action against common threats faced by both NATO and Russia and was set up to serve as the main forum for advancing NATO-Russian relations. It was designed to give the NATO-Russia partnership new impetus and substance over the previous PJC. Within the NRC, the allies and Russia work together as equal partners to identify and pursue opportunities for joint action, regularly consulting on current security issues and developing practical cooperation in a wide range of areas of common interest.[18]

Specifically, the council works on the basis of continuous political dialogue on security issues to identify early on any emerging problems, determine common approaches, and conduct joint operations as appropriate.[19] The NRC laid out an ambitious plan. According to the Rome Declaration,

> the NATO-Russia Council will provide a mechanism for consultation, consensus-building, cooperation, joint decision, and joint action for the

member states of NATO and Russia on a wide spectrum of security issues in the Euro-Atlantic region. The NATO-Russia Council will serve as the principal structure and venue for advancing the relationship between NATO and Russia. It will operate on the principle of consensus. . . . NATO member states and Russia will continue to intensify their cooperation in areas including the struggle against terrorism, crisis management, non-proliferation, arms control and confidence-building measures, theater missile defense, search and rescue at sea, military-to-military cooperation, and civil emergencies.[20]

Comprising three committees, seven standing working groups, and a number of other ad hoc expert groups designed to develop further cooperation in key areas, the NRC goes far beyond the previous PJC by seating Russia equally "at 27" with the 26 allies for open, transparent discussions, rather than having the allies first arrive at consensus and then face Russia later with a consolidated front. This arrangement has allowed Russia to take part in discussions as much more of a partner-in-fact, and has been far more satisfactory to Moscow than the previous "NATO + 1" format under the PJC.[21] Furthermore, as with the North Atlantic Council, decisions taken by the NATO-Russia Council are made on the basis of consensus.[22]

One of the biggest advantages for Russia of the NRC over the previous PJC is that Russia can now see firsthand frank discussion and even disagreements among NATO allies. Although that raises the prospect of Russia potentially taking advantage of these differences to try to drive a wedge between NATO members, it also gives Russia the benefit of participating in actual, genuine debate and discussion with alliance members over policies and actions, which it clearly did not have under the previous structure.

The NRC also now involves far more areas and organizations than did the PJC. The council involves a wide variety of professionals, including intelligence officers, border guards, interior ministry troops, and civil-emergency planning experts. In addition, Russian scientists have made regular and substantial contributions to the NRC and, significantly, the Russian mission to NATO is now no longer just an adjunct of the Russian Embassy to Belgium. After years of formalities and stiff coordination, the alliance and Russia finally feel much more like partners.[23]

Notes

(Most of the notes in this and the following chapters appear in shortened form. For full details, see the appropriate entries in the bibliography.)

1. "NATO-Russia Relations," *NATO Issues.*
2. Bennett, "Building Effective Partnerships," 22.
3. "The Euro-Atlantic Partnership," *NATO Topics.*
4. The policies NATO established through the PfP have resulted in one of the alliance's great post–Cold War successes, as the policies have been steadily extended in order to build more effective relationships with a wide variety of countries and international institutions. See "Expanding Operations."
5. "Growing NATO-Russian Cooperation," 125–26.
6. Mroziewicz, "Enlargement and the Capabilities Gap," 79.
7. "Alliance's Strategic Concept," 12.
8. *NATO Transformed,* 20.
9. "NATO-Russia Relations," *NATO Issues.*
10. "Alliance's Strategic Concept," 11.
11. Burns, "NATO-Russia Council."
12. Fritch, "NATO's Strategic Partnerships."
13. Ibid.
14. *NATO-Russia: Forging Deeper Relations,* 7.
15. Article V is the core clause of NATO's founding charter, which states that an armed attack against one ally shall be considered an attack against them all. In response to an invocation of Article V, each ally determines, in consultation with other allies, how it can best contribute to any action deemed necessary to restore and maintain the security of the North Atlantic area, including the use of armed force. See *NATO Transformed,* 5.
16. Robertson, "Introduction," 5.
17. Powell, "Powell Sees Bright Future."
18. "NATO-Russia Relations," *NATO Issues.*
19. Meetings of the NRC are chaired by NATO's secretary general and are held at least monthly at the level of ambassadors and military representatives, twice yearly at the level of foreign and defense ministers and chiefs of staff, and occasionally at summit level. Another important innovation under the NRC is the Preparatory Committee, which meets at least twice monthly to prepare ambassadorial discussions and to oversee all experts' activities under the auspices of the NRC. See "NATO-Russia Council."
20. "NATO-Russia Relations: A New Quality," 6–7. See also "NATO-Russia Council."
21. The NRC working groups and committees focus on cooperation on terrorism, proliferation, peacekeeping, theater missile defense, airspace management, civil emergencies, defense reform, logistics, scientific cooperation, and challenges of modern society. See "NATO-Russia Council" and also "NATO-Russia Relations."
22. "NATO in the 21st Century," 13.
23. Fritch, "NATO's Strategic Partnerships."

Chapter 3

Russian Responses and Perspectives

A nation has neither permanent enemies nor friends, only permanent interests.

—Charles de Gaulle

While Russia has accepted NATO's expansion thus far and is consulting with the allies in the NRC, the Kremlin nonetheless has continued to express its view that enlargement of the alliance is both unnecessary and unhelpful in furthering Euro-Atlantic security. In its view, other international bodies and organizations are perfectly suited to take on the role of collective security that NATO has grown into over the past few years. President Putin, in his remarks at the Rome Summit, made clear the Russian position that other international agreements and bodies will also play a critical role in supporting the new NATO-Russian relationship under the NRC, stating,

> Russia is primarily interested in it as a working instrument. It is of fundamental importance that cooperation at twenty should be based on a firm foundation of international law—the UN Charter, the Helsinki Final Act and the OSCE [Organization for Security and Cooperation in Europe] Charter on European Security. . . . For Russia, with its geopolitical position, the enhancement of cooperation with NATO as equal partners is one of the real embodiments of the multiple approach, to which there is no alternative and which we intend to pursue resolutely. We do not think of ourselves as outside Europe, but it is also unthinkable for us that the role of approved cooperation mechanisms in Asia and in the Commonwealth of Independent States should be underestimated. Only by harmoniously combining our actions in all these areas will we open up wide-ranging possibilities for building a single security region—from Vancouver to Vladivostok.[1]

Thus, the Russian government acknowledges publicly that working with NATO is useful and beneficial for both Russia and the alliance in the interest of overall security. The Russian mission to NATO has certainly "toed the party line" and acknowledged this as well. Gen Konstantin Totskiy, Russia's first ambassador to NATO, elaborated in an interview that "the days of confrontation are past and Russians no longer associate NATO with the enemy. Quite the reverse. In recent years, people have come to understand that the common threats and challenges of the modern world call for ever-closer cooperation."[2]

Popular Misconceptions of NATO Intent

Privately, however, Russian suspicion still runs deep when considering its former foe from beyond the Fulda Gap. NATO is by far the least popular of all international organizations among the general Russian population. Polls conducted after the latest round of NATO enlargement in 2004 suggest that approximately 52 percent of Russians believe NATO enlargement threatens Russia's national interests, while 58 percent believe that NATO is an aggressive military bloc.[3] Most Russians believe the United Nations is the best international body for global cooperation, the Organization for Security and Cooperation in Europe (OSCE) for nonmilitary crisis management in Eastern European crisis regions, the EU for economic matters, and the United States for strategic partnership, despite recent challenges to that relationship.[4]

Russians still generally dislike NATO and almost anything it stands for. In the words of Rolf Welberts, director of NATO's information office in Moscow, many Russians still consider NATO "an illegitimate, US-dominated remnant of the Cold War, a potentially aggressive military bloc the world would be better off without."[5] Many Russians still mirror-image NATO with the previous Soviet-dominated Warsaw Pact and remain highly skeptical of the idea that the United States does not dominate NATO, despite the recent, very public disagreements among the allies over the war in Iraq.

NATO secretary general Jaap de Hoop Scheffer has tried valiantly to dispel those perceptions. In Moscow in April 2004, he reiterated that the recent addition of seven new NATO members was not aimed against Russia and that the alliance wants to cooperate with Russia to address global threats. He stated in a Moscow radio interview, "I consider it my job, my responsibility, to convince (Russians) that NATO has no ulterior motives. NATO wants to cooperate. NATO needs Russia and Russia needs NATO. We live in a dangerous world and we can only solve these problems together."[6]

The United States has also continued to try to reassure Russia that it has nothing to fear from further enlargement of the alliance. Secretary of State Colin Powell reiterated in April 2004 that President George W. Bush has given repeated assurances that "you're not our enemies anymore," and any concerns about NATO enlargement near Russia's borders are groundless.[7]

Although perceptions are slow to change, there is still room for hope and progress following the opening of the NATO Information Office in 2001. One of its many successes has been the creation of a NATO column in the newspaper *Krasnaya Zvezda* (*Red Star*), the official newspaper of the Russian armed forces and one that is traditionally very critical of the alliance.[8] The fact that this newspaper allows a commentary by an "adversary" such as NATO does indeed point to no small progress, no matter how far there is still to go in the relationship.

Economic Conditions and Realities

Russia is definitely struggling with its own economy, particularly since the fall of 1998, and the state of disrepair throughout the Russian armed forces is shocking. The author noted this sad state of affairs shortly after arriving at the US Embassy in Moscow in the summer of 2000, when the *Kursk* submarine tragedy occurred.[9] Although this particular mishap highlighted the condition of the Russian navy, it was also indicative of the state of the other services in Russia's forces. President Putin has taken several tangible steps to try to correct the problem, but it will be a long time before Russia's forces regain very much of their former strength and pride. Russia simply does not have the money or ready resources that the former Soviet Union once had.

Russia is looking hard for whatever resources it does still own to help rebuild its flagging economy. In particular, Russia's natural resources and its arms sales to other countries, especially China and India, are major sources of continuing revenue. Moscow is also putting on a "full-court press" to try to integrate further into European and international economic structures, such as the World Trade Organization (WTO) and the EU. Conventional wisdom currently holds that Russia's prospects for EU membership are slim to none, at least in the near future. As a senior US administration official stated at a press conference just prior to the February 2004 NATO Summit in Brussels, "The question of Russia's membership in the European Union is not only hypothetical, it is more than that—it is somewhat beyond hypothetical at the present time. And that really isn't on anyone's agenda, including Russia's."[10]

Russia's prospects for entry into the WTO rate somewhat higher. President Bush recently expressed support for closer integration of the Russian Federation into European and Western organizations. During his February 2005 address to the EU at Concert Noble in Brussels, he stated that he believes "Russia's future lies within the family of Europe and the transatlantic community. America supports WTO membership for Russia, because meeting WTO standards will strengthen the gains of freedom and prosperity in that country."[11]

However, this strong support comes with a price. For the United States, continued progress toward greater democratization and reform is paramount to show genuine commitment on Russia's part to join the international family of democratic nations. President Bush also pointed out in Brussels that "for Russia to make progress as a European nation, the Russian government must renew a commitment to democracy and the rule of law. We recognize that reform will not happen overnight. We must always remind Russia, however, that our alliance stands for a free press, a vital opposition, the sharing of power, and the rule of law—and the United States and all European countries should place democratic reform at the heart of their dialogue with Russia."[12]

Philosophical Internal Debate— To Westernize or Not?

The Russian people have struggled for centuries to define their identity and place in the world. As an enormous empire and still the world's geographically largest country by far—even after the dissolution of the Soviet Union—Russia straddles the European and Asian continents in more than just a physical sense. Throughout Russia's incredibly rich history, outside influences have had profound impacts on its development as a society, culture, and nation—sometimes violently and sometimes gradually. One of the biggest internal debates Russians themselves have had over the centuries has centered on whether to "Westernize" or to "remain true to Mother Russia," pure and undefiled by outside influences. This is a question Russia has struggled with almost from its very beginnings and more so during the past 300 years, especially as Europe modernized and progressed. Peter the Great was one of the earliest "Westernizers," and strongly pushed his country toward Europe, to the point of founding St. Petersburg as his "window on the West."[13]

The empire eventually spread to the Pacific Ocean, and Russia's crest shows a double-headed eagle for a very good reason—it symbolizes the czar's (and now the president's) watchful eye over both continents of the Russian Empire, Europe and Asia. Russia was and is both European and Asian, and will not fall completely into either camp, nor forsake either continent's legacy. As much as Russia feels itself to be a part of a larger Europe, it also considers itself to be a global and Eurasian power. Ivan Ivanov, a former deputy Russian foreign minister, very well summed up the Russian view that, "While stressing our European identity we prefer to have a free hand in our policy towards and cooperation with all regions, including Asia, the United States, and above all, the CIS [Commonwealth of Independent States]."[14]

The double-headed eagle on the Russian crest not only signifies the czar's watchful eye over both directions of his vast empire, it may also symbolize the Russian soul, torn between East and West. The result is that in many ways, Russians feel that they do not belong fully to East or West, and thus have their own special history and calling in the world. Though many in the West view this as simply a philosophical or even spiritual outlook having little to do with tangible realities, it actually resonates at the heart of the Russian soul and colors the way Russians look at the rest of the world. NATO is now seeing the results of this outlook as it seeks to grow eastward and must now find more and more creative ways to assuage Russian fears and distrust.

At present Russia is still interested in pursuing continuing closer ties with NATO and Europe in general. Andrei Kelin, deputy director of the Department of General European Cooperation in the Russian Ministry of Foreign Affairs, recently shed some light on Moscow's thinking in this regard. He described NATO as "one of the main European community institutions, and if we want to steer a course for normal relations with each community state, which, properly speaking, we have sought to do lately, it will be logical to form civilized working ties with all key European organizations, NATO included."[15] The importance of NATO capitalizing on this sentiment through continued close cooperation with Russia cannot be overstated.

Notes

1. Putin, "Address," 18.
2. Totskiy, "Interview."
3. Kuznetsova, "NATO," 22.
4. Welberts, "Explaining NATO."
5. Ibid.
6. de Hoop Scheffer, "NATO, Russia Enhance Military Cooperation."
7. Powell, "Russia Need Not Worry."
8. Welberts, "Explaining NATO."
9. The author served as assistant air attaché and air attaché at the US Embassy in Moscow from June 2000 to June 2002.
10. "NATO Lauded as 'Centerpiece'," *United States Mission to NATO.*
11. Bush, "President Discusses American and European Alliance."
12. Ibid.
13. MacKenzie and Curran, *History of Russia,* 197–98.
14. *Twain Shall Meet,* 37.
15. Kelin, "Attitude to NATO Expansion," 17.

Chapter 4

Contentious Issues

Any extension of the zone of NATO is unacceptable.

—Mikhail S. Gorbachev, 1990

In light of these issues, NATO and Russia still face significant challenges to their relationship. This chapter examines a number of these contentious issues and highlights their root causes, for it is these causes that continue to plague the alliance in its relations with Russia. These issues are highlighted due to their underlying sources of friction and disagreements, problems that both sides can expect to continue into future years and that must be dealt with to make it possible for NATO and Russia to continue working together productively. Chapter 6 addresses several recommendations for the alliance leadership as it strives first to understand, and second, to work effectively with Russia in its decision-making process.

NATO Expansion

Russian leaders publicly maintain they have no official objection to NATO's recent expansions (NATO has now had five enlargements since its inception in 1949—see figure below for a timeline of all expansions to date). In May 2002, at the opening of the NATO Military Liaison Mission in Moscow, then-first deputy chief of the General Staff (now chief), Col-Gen Yuri Baluyevsky, stated that Russia "does not fear NATO's expansion if its new members do not threaten its national security and use their infrastructure to deploy strategic arms." He went on to explain that Russia's policy has become more predictable and that Russia does not threaten any other nation, but he also added significantly that it has defended and will defend its national sovereignty.[1]

However, the true underlying Russian position on NATO expansion is clear and not surprising—Russia does not support it. Russian concerns center around the prospect of facing potential new military bases, military units, and the infrastructure of

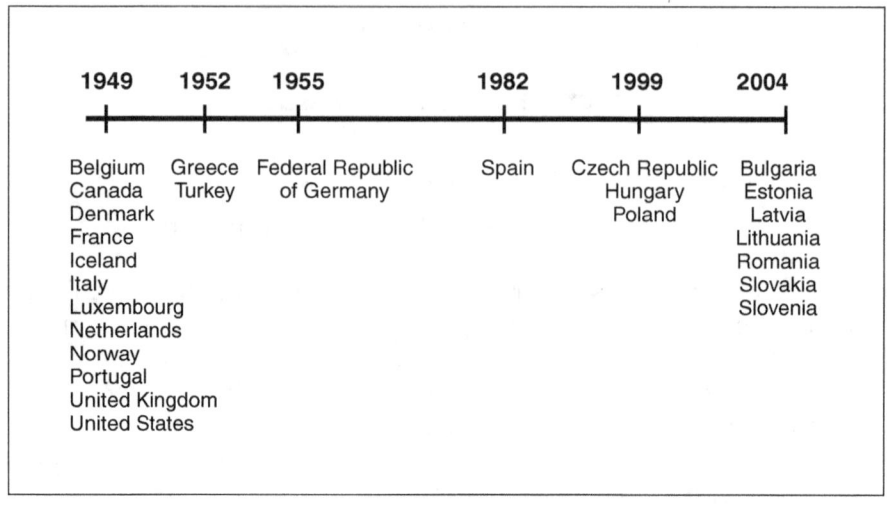

1949	1952	1955	1982	1999	2004

Belgium Greece Federal Republic   Spain   Czech Republic Bulgaria
Canada Turkey   of Germany   Hungary   Estonia
Denmark   Poland   Latvia
France   Lithuania
Iceland   Romania
Italy   Slovakia
Luxembourg   Slovenia
Netherlands
Norway
Portugal
United Kingdom
United States

Timeline of NATO Enlargement. Adapted from *Istanbul Summit Reader's Guide* (Brussels: NATO Office of Information and Press, 2004), 120–21.

a powerful military alliance right on its borders. Russian opinion holds this to be an "echo of the past, a relic of the Cold War," and Moscow clearly favors more universal security mechanisms for the Euro-Atlantic area, such as the United Nations and the Organization for Security and Cooperation in Europe. Despite NATO's many assurances to Russia, Moscow continues automatically to view with suspicion any expansion farther eastward. There also remains a persistent belief that one of the main reasons for NATO's expansion was to contribute to the weakening of Russia, which began in the early 1990s with the dissolution of the Soviet Union.[2] As General Totskiy understated it, "We do not consider NATO's further enlargement to be a cause for celebration."[3]

Russian concerns over NATO expansion only deepened after the most recent round brought the Baltic republics, which physically border Russia, into the NATO fold. It is true that Russia lodged no strenuous, lasting objections to either of the two most recent rounds of NATO expansion. However, this was undoubtedly more due to Russian preoccupation with pressing domestic and internal issues—such as their economy and challenges with their own version of terrorism originating in their southern regions—as well as the fact that most of the new NATO members did not physically border Russia (with the exception of the small Baltic republics). As US ambassador to Russia Alexander Vershbow pointed out recently at Princeton University, the Russian reaction, while "not enthusiastic, was not negative as some had expected."[4]

Future Enlargement

That reaction, however, undoubtedly will not continue to be the case when NATO prepares to offer future membership to more former Soviet satellite countries in another round of enlargement, which is expected to occur within the next few years. At the June 2004 Istanbul Summit, NATO leaders made it clear that they intended to "leave the door wide open" to any country wishing to join and able to meet its entry requirements, and that the seven countries that had just joined would not be the last. To that end, they welcomed progress toward membership made by Albania, Croatia, and the former Yugoslav Republic of Macedonia in the framework of the Membership Action Plan (MAP).[5] Secretary of State Powell reiterated this view a few months later following his last North Atlantic Council meeting in December 2004, stating,

> to become a member of NATO is to coordinate and connect yourself to all of Europe. But not just Europe. You connect yourself in a very important way to North America, to the United States and Canada. That's why the Alliance is thriving. That's why more and more nations want to become part of this great Alliance. So, I see a bright future for NATO. . . . There are more nations out there waiting for their turn to join the Alliance: an Alliance that continues to grow, that continues to have the complete commitment of its original members and the new energy of its new members and aspiring members as an Alliance that will continue to be valuable, continue to be vital, as part of the transatlantic family partnership.[6]

In addition to the three candidates mentioned above, the alliance will also very likely consider Georgia, Moldova, and even Ukraine, a country to which Russia has far stronger strategic and historical ties. According to former US ambassador to NATO Nicholas Burns, the alliance is reaching out to the region as it establishes, "for the very first time, liaison offices in the

Caucasus and Central Asian region, and that reflects the increased cooperation with the countries of those regions." He also reiterated NATO's desire to engage Ukraine, particularly following that country's December 2004 presidential election (more on this below). Keeping in mind Russian sensitivities, he spoke of making an attempt to give more attention to NATO-Russian relations and to strengthen those relations, adding that "there's reason to think that we have a lot more that we can do with Russia in terms of our partnership."[7] However, if membership expands to several more countries bordering Russia, that partnership will surely be sorely tested.

Of course, the Central and Eastern European countries being considered for membership are eagerly anticipating that possibility. They still have a tendency to view NATO as a sort of US tool for protecting its European partners against military aggression from third parties, mainly Russia. This view is understandable, given the role the former Soviet Union played in dominating the Warsaw Pact. However, it does not accurately reflect today's reality, and NATO's challenge is to help Central and Eastern European countries realize there is much more to NATO membership than developing relations with just one or even a few new partners, rather than with the entire alliance.[8]

NATO continues, however, to lay the groundwork for potential new aspirants in the next probable round of expansion. According to the Georgian Foreign Ministry, the secretary general's newly appointed special representative for Caucasus and Central Asian countries, Robert Simmons, visited Georgia in early February 2005 to hold talks with the Georgian president, prime minister, state minister for Euro-Atlantic Integration issues, foreign minister, and other top-level Georgian officials. Significantly, the North Atlantic Council in October 2004 approved Georgia's Individual Partnership Action Plan (IPAP), which establishes specific defense and political reform goals for Georgia. The next month, NATO secretary general de Hoop Scheffer paid a one-day visit to Georgia, saying that "Georgia matters for the [sic] NATO," and calling on the Georgian authorities to implement the IPAP.[9]

Georgia has responded by raising the stakes recently in its overtures toward NATO by insisting in ever-stronger terms that Russian forces vacate their bases in Georgia. On 10 March

2005, the Georgian Parliament voted 159 to 0 to urge the Georgian government to set a deadline for Moscow to close two Russian military bases, again highlighting the long-standing dispute between the two countries. This is only one of several issues that have been sore spots between the two governments since Georgia's "Rose Revolution" in November 2003, and will not likely disappear until Russian forces leave and the question of South Ossetia is finally resolved.[10]

In light of this likely third round of enlargement into what Moscow considers its immediate sphere of influence, Russian mistrust will surely only deepen, and their protests (and response) will undoubtedly grow more strident. The Kremlin already has a hard time accepting that former Warsaw Pact members it once dominated are now members of NATO and enjoy the privilege of NATO Article 5 protection. Any expansion that includes the Caucasus and especially Ukraine will, in Moscow's view, directly threaten its influence over an area that it perceives to be its own and that borders the Russian Federation. This is particularly true in view of the fact that the Russian Empire had its beginnings in Kievan Rus (current-day Ukraine) as far back as the ninth century.[11]

The Special Case of Ukraine

NATO-Ukrainian relations were formally launched in 1991, when Ukraine joined the North Atlantic Cooperation Council immediately after achieving independence following the breakup of the Soviet Union. In 1994 Ukraine became the first of the Commonwealth of Independent States to join the Partnership for Peace program and subsequently demonstrated its commitment to contribute to NATO-led peacekeeping operations in the Balkans.[12] By 1997 the two sides had signed the NATO-Ukraine Charter on a Distinctive Partnership in Madrid, which recognized the importance of an independent, stable, and democratic Ukraine to European stability. That same year, the alliance established a NATO Information and Documentation Center in Kyiv to facilitate wider access to information on NATO, particularly in the post–Cold War era and concerning Ukrainian benefits from their distinctive partnership. Two years later, in 1999, NATO

21

opened a liaison office in Kyiv to help Ukraine's participation in the PfP and to support Ukrainian defense reform efforts.[13]

Ukrainian leadership has made several overtures toward NATO. On the eve of the 1999 50th anniversary NATO celebration, then-Ukrainian president Leonid Kuchma spoke in glowing terms of this new relationship, saying, "The Ukraine-NATO distinctive partnership is important and indispensable to the new European security architecture," and that "there is no doubt that these events will not only open a new page in the 50-year history of the Alliance, but [also will] foreshadow a new stage in the dynamic development of the Ukraine-NATO distinctive partnership, all on behalf of Euro-Atlantic security and stability."[14] Kuchma later declared boldly in May 2002, just before the fifth anniversary of the Distinctive Partnership, that Ukraine now had the goal of eventual NATO membership.[15] The alliance responded later that same month, agreeing to explore ways to take the NATO-Ukrainian relationship to a qualitatively new level beyond their previous support, where they had already cited the importance of Ukrainian "sovereignty and independence, territorial integrity, democratic development, economic prosperity and its status as a non-nuclear weapons state as key factors of stability and security in central and eastern Europe and in Europe as a whole."[16]

Ukrainian president Viktor Yushchenko also has made clear his plans to integrate further into Europe's various structures and organizations. At the Brussels Summit, he thanked the alliance for its support during his election ordeal, saying,

> our declarations, which correspond to our actions, a course of integration in the European and Euro-Atlantic structures, from now on will determine the strategy and tactics of our policy. We believe that Ukraine's participation and engagement in the North Atlantic community of democratic peoples will strengthen peace and security on the European continent. We are ready to make all necessary efforts to achieve this noble goal. We have already created a strong foundation for our mutual relations and can extend it. . . . The European future of Ukraine is inseparably linked with the deepening of its relationship with the Alliance.[17]

From the alliance's perspective, there is now renewed interest in Ukraine's prospects for drawing closer to NATO. US secretary of state Condoleezza Rice stated at a February 2005 press conference in Brussels, "We look very much forward to continuing to work with Ukraine as it develops its democratic future." She reminded her audience that "Ukraine has an action plan with NATO that we can be more active on now, and we should do exactly that so that we begin to take the practical steps that can support Ukraine's democratic process and can support Ukraine's coming toward Europe and toward mainstream Europe."[18]

At a press background briefing in Brussels just prior to the February NATO-Ukraine Summit, a senior US administration official candidly acknowledged that "the general attitude within NATO . . . is that NATO ought to be open to a new relationship with Ukraine. That is going to be focused, at this point, on fulfilling a partnership plan that we developed with the Ukrainians a couple of years ago. We didn't make much progress on that, for obvious reason, given the politics in Ukraine over the last year. But there's strong hope that in 2005 we might deepen our partnership with Ukraine."[19]

Other NATO leaders also reaffirmed this commitment to Ukraine during the summit, saying the alliance leadership "pledged continued support and welcomed their aspirations for building a democratic and prosperous Ukraine and strengthening their integration into the Euro-Atlantic community."[20] Secretary General de Hoop Scheffer elaborated even further during the summit when he mentioned the PfP trust fund project that was about to be launched to help Ukraine deal with old ammunition, small arms, and light-weapons stockpiles—the largest initiative of its kind ever undertaken. He addressed President Yushchenko directly and declared, "NATO is ready to work with you, to support you, and to help you build a better future. All Allies are committed—are fully committed, to a rich and progressively stronger partnership with Ukraine."[21]

Ukraine, however, still faces some difficult decisions balancing its potential membership in NATO with the necessity of maintaining its relationship with Russia. Due to geopolitics and centuries of intertwined economics, culture, and history, Ukraine and Russia have been and will continue to be inextricably linked into the future. This point was brought home shortly after the breakup of the Soviet Union during a visit to Ukraine by the then head of the US Information Agency, Amb. Henry Catto. While Catto was meeting with Ukrainian Minister of Culture Larysa Khorolets and Foreign Minister Anatoliy

Zlenko, Khorolets stated clearly that "Russia is our partner—our equal partner. We may differ, but they are our neighbors and we are linked economically."[22]

Even with EU and NATO aspirations, this view from the windows of Kyiv toward their northern neighbor has not changed substantially. President Yushchenko most recently addressed Ukraine's relationship to Russia, even as he pushed further for NATO membership. Despite Russia's recent blatant and distasteful meddling in the 2004 Ukrainian presidential election, Yushchenko was still able to say, "I would like to clearly state once again that Russia is our strategic partner and Ukraine's policy towards NATO by any means will be against [viewed in consideration of] the interests of other countries, including Russia."[23]

NATO's Changing Roles and Missions

NATO's own roles and missions also are evolving with the ever-changing strategic world environment. In a recent speech to the Atlantic Treaty Association's (ATA) 50th General Assembly in Rome, Secretary General de Hoop Scheffer emphasized that this new environment needs the broadest possible international cooperation. He pointed out that this cooperation is "the heart of the 'wide web' of international security, including NATO's dialogue with Ukraine and Russia." He went on to also clarify that NATO's responsibility is no longer simply Euro-centric territorial defense. In his view, NATO will continue to have out-of-area operations, such as those now going on in Afghanistan and, to a limited extent, Iraq.[24]

Gen James Jones, supreme allied commander Europe (SACEUR), also discussed the changing NATO focus at the ATA General Assembly when he stated that NATO is undergoing the "most fundamental transformation in its history." The goal of NATO, he said, is to be "as relevant in the 21st century as it was in the 20th century."[25] Certainly, Russian leaders who hear these statements come to the only logical conclusion that NATO has no intention of disbanding, or even of merging with another international security body, such as the OSCE, which Russia would much prefer. The message is that NATO is here to stay and will continue to adapt and change to the world around it, much to the chagrin of Kremlin leadership.

NATO also will continue to maintain a presence in former Yugoslav territories in the Balkans, primarily in Kosovo. Alliance leaders reiterated this intent in a joint statement during the February 2005 NATO Summit in Brussels. According to the statement, "We remain firm in our commitment to stability in the Balkans and see the future of this region firmly anchored in the Euro-Atlantic community. NATO will maintain its strong presence in Kosovo and contribute to the UN-led political process of building a multiethnic, peaceful and prosperous society."[26] As it is a historically Slav-dominated region ("Yugoslav" means "southern Slav" in Russian and Serbo-Croatian), Russia is undoubtedly less than thrilled with this continuing alliance presence in this contentious area.

Air Policing

When the 10 most recent aspirants became full NATO members in 1999 and 2004, they immediately fell under NATO's formal collective security and defense umbrella, which still happens to include routine policing of all NATO airspace as required. Historically, all alliance members have either performed their own air-policing functions or fulfilled the mission in cooperation with neighboring NATO nations. Of the most recent seven adherents, Romania, Bulgaria, and Slovakia have their own defense capabilities, and Slovenian airspace will be covered by a combination of its own early warning system and air-policing support provided by the Italian air force. However, the Baltic states of Estonia, Latvia, and Lithuania—the only ones physically bordering Russia—called on NATO to provide initial air policing over the extended NATO skies. As a result, in March 2004, four NATO F-16 aircraft began a rotating deployment to Estonia to provide the same level of routine security as for all alliance members, sparking vigorous protests from the Russian government.[27]

Although the alliance's new air-policing operation over the Baltic states initially caused bitter complaints from Moscow, especially from the Duma (the Russian parliament), these concerns were eventually assuaged. The new policy was justified to Russia as a deterrent to would-be terrorists and other "renegades" who might try to enter the European continent's air-

25

space illegally through the Baltics. Furthermore, Moscow could not realistically argue that four NATO F-16s were a threat to the entire Russian armed forces or to Russia's well-being or sovereignty. Secretary of State Powell gave strong assurances that the deployment of these fighters was in no way directed against Russia, asserting that NATO would "adjust to the new threats that are out there. We're not worried about the old threat of the Soviet Union." He also noted the Russian government still has an obligation to make sure its armed forces are defending the Russian Federation, stating "they are passionate about that and they have to reflect the public opinion and the intellectual opinion that exists within Russia." The Russians now seem to have accepted the deployment and, in the words of Secretary Powell, are "taking it in stride."[28]

Future East European Basing Options

In conjunction with Russian fears about NATO's eastward growth, the Kremlin is particularly concerned about the future possibility that NATO will base its soldiers on the territory of the newest NATO members. Admittedly, it is problematic when Russia sees active plans for NATO forces to be stationed on former Warsaw Pact soil. For example, plans are already under way to create a Joint Force Training Center in Poland. NATO is using this facility, along with other arrangements, to initiate a complete overhaul of alliance training under the direction of the Allied Command Transformation, based in Norfolk, Virginia.[29]

NATO, on the other hand, has downplayed the plans and tried to convince Russia those plans are not directed against the Russian Federation. NATO leaders insist the planned troop deployment does not mean NATO is trying to surround Russia with more troops. The United States in particular is doing just the opposite and is leading the Western effort to "downsize" through its own defense transformation. Secretary Powell put it succinctly when he stated that the United States is "not putting more troops in to surround Russia" but rather "moving troops out of Europe even more than we've moved over the last 10 or 12 years," which has been significant in itself.[30] However, the general Russian public remains unconvinced.

Other Political Challenges

NATO (particularly the United States) and Russia still have fundamental disagreements over the Conventional Forces in Europe (CFE) Treaty, which has not yet been ratified years after the end of the Cold War. The Western position is that the treaty will not be submitted for ratification until Russia complies with stipulations to remove its armed forces from Georgia and Moldova. Russia now is using recent NATO accessions to argue that the spirit of the CFE Treaty has the potential to be violated, particularly considering the new status of the Baltic republics as NATO members. As General Totskiy pointedly stated,

> Russia's legitimate security interests must be taken into account. We realize that the seven states invited to join NATO will not increase the alliance's overall military capabilities by much. But in terms of infrastructure and geography, the potential for NATO deployments is increasing. Moreover, NATO membership for the Baltic countries, which border Russia, brings with it a host of unresolved issues that directly affect our interests. At present, for example, there are no force-deployment limitations in the Baltic Republics under the Treaty on Conventional Forces in Europe. In effect, this means that this territory could become an "arms-control-free zone." I think that the way Russians view NATO will largely depend on how this issue is resolved.[31]

Furthermore, Russia is taking an opportunity to counter NATO moves by expanding its own influence and presence with countries near its borders, particularly in Central Asia. In October 2003, President Putin and Kyrgyzstan president Askar Akayev signed an agreement within the framework of the Collective Security Treaty Organization regarding the stationing of a Russian air base in Kant. According to Col-Gen Yevgeny Yuryev, the commander of the Ural Air Force and Air Defense Combined Formation, the declared purpose of the agreement with Kyrgyzstan was to reinforce the "unified security system" in Central Asia with SU-25 attack aircraft and military transport helicopters. Currently, 250 personnel are stationed at the base, with plans for a considerable increase and assignment of more-modern SU-27 fighter aircraft. This action also corresponds to the reorganization of the 201st Motorized Rifle Division, already stationed in Tajikistan, as a full military base.[32]

Finally, the eventual status of Kosovo remains a challenging thorn in the sides of both Russia and the West, and the Kremlin is keeping a keen eye on events in the Balkans. While Kosovo is still formally a part of Serbia, the long-standing battle over its self-determination versus Belgrade's sovereignty has strong implications for numerous semi-autonomous regions throughout the Russian Federation. In particular, Moscow is concerned about "rebel" separatist actions in Abkhazia, South Ossetia, and especially Chechnya. Growing NATO (or other Western) involvement in these and other areas has already drawn Kremlin criticism of the West's intentions and will likely continue until the issue is satisfactorily resolved for all interested parties.

Notes

1. Baluyevsky, "General Baluyevsky."
2. Troitski, *Transatlantic Union*, 146.
3. Totskiy, "Interview."
4. Vershbow, "United States and Russia."
5. "NATO's Open Door," 119. The MAP offers aspiring members practical advice and targeted assistance. In turn aspiring members are expected to meet certain political goals, including the peaceful resolution of territorial disputes, respect for democratic procedures and the rule of law, and the democratic control of their armed forces. Participation in the plan does not offer any guarantee of future membership, but it does help countries to adapt their armed forces and to prepare for the obligations and responsibilities alliance membership would bring. See "NATO in the 21st Century," 14.
6. Powell, "Powell Sees Bright Future."
7. Burns, "Pre-Ministerial Briefing."
8. Mroziewicz, "Enlargement and the Capabilities Gap," 91.
9. de Hoop Scheffer, "NATO Envoy to Visit Georgia."
10. "Vote in Parliament," 6.
11. MacKenzie and Curran, *History of Russia*, 24.
12. "Further Developing NATO-Ukraine Relations," 130–31.
13. "New Relationships," 44.
14. Kuchma, "Message from Leonid Kuchma," 49.
15. *NATO-Ukraine*, 2.
16. "Alliance's Strategic Concept," 12.
17. Yushchenko, "Opening Statement at the Meeting of the NATO-Ukraine Council."
18. Rice, "Remarks at the North Atlantic Treaty Organization Headquarters."
19. "NATO Lauded as 'Centerpiece'," *United States Mission to NATO*.
20. "Statement Issued by the Heads of State," *NATO On-Line Library*.
21. de Hoop Scheffer, "Opening Statement at the Press Conference." See also de Hoop Scheffer, "Opening Remarks."
22. Catto, *Ambassadors at Sea*, 333.
23. Yushchenko, "Opening Statement."
24. de Hoop Scheffer, address.

25. Jones, address.
26. "Statement Issued by the Heads of State."
27. "Air Policing over the Baltics."
28. Powell, "Russia Need Not Worry."
29. Stanhope, address.
30. Powell, "Russia Need Not Worry."
31. Totskiy, "Interview."
32. Yuryev, "Kant Air Base."

Chapter 5

Areas of Cooperation

A second marriage is a triumph of hope over experience, all the more so when the partners are the same.

—Anonymous

Closer Political Integration

Despite the significant challenges and obstacles still facing the alliance and Russia, both sides have seen the need to cooperate more fully in areas of mutual security concern and have dedicated themselves to working more closely together, particularly over the past two years. Although President Putin has repeatedly made clear that he has no intention of joining NATO, he has made good relations with NATO a personal priority.[1] General Totskiy related that before he left for Brussels, President Putin summoned him and instructed him that "NATO is now a serious and important organization with a visible role to play in international affairs," and with which Russia needs to have "effective working relations."[2] Sergey Rogov, director of the Institute for US and Canadian Studies at the Russian Academy of Sciences, has elaborated further on the distinction drawn by Putin—the key issue is Russia's relationship with NATO, not Russia's role in NATO.[3]

The United States has also emphasized that close relations with Russia are important, within the alliance as well as on a bilateral basis. During Secretary of State Rice's February 2005 trip to Europe, she stated that "we are in complete agreement that there are trends in Russia that need to be watched, that we are concerned that Russia's isolation would be a terrible thing for the international community, and that we intend to continue to work with our Russian colleagues for a better future."[4] Ambassador Burns has also pointed out the value of Russian relations with NATO, an organization he calls the "most effective vehicle for multilateral action available to Europe, the U.S., and Canada," and that "brings together the

31

NATO Allies and the Partnership nations—Russia, Ukraine, and our friends in Central Asia and the Caucasus—in a way that reinforces the common values we share."[5] He further asserted that "the U.S. certainly recognizes that a healthy, democratic Russia is in its long-term strategic interest. . . . The logic behind NATO's partnership with Russia is, therefore, not 'zero-sum.' It is 'win-win.' We realize we can accomplish much more together than we can apart." The key will be to "overcome our differences, and to recognize the strength of our collective bond."[6]

Improved Consultation—NATO-Russia Council (NRC) and Military Liaison Missions

Despite the two most recent rounds of expansion, Russia nonetheless has drawn closer to NATO through the NRC, and the council is continuing to make noticeable strides toward better NATO-Russian cooperation. Ambassador Burns reinforced this view when he noted, "The Council is only just beginning to hit its stride as an effective security partnership—it will grow in stature and influence as NATO and Russia eventually overcome remaining Cold War stereotypes and strengthen their developing military and political ties."[7] General Totskiy also asserted that NATO-Russian cooperation was a priority for Russia. He has said Russia is convinced that by further enhancing cooperation with NATO across the entire range of areas set out in the Rome Declaration, Russia will be able to make a major contribution to the evolution of a new security architecture in the Euro-Atlantic area (a major Russian goal, to be sure) and that the NRC will be one of the leading elements of such an architecture.[8]

The aftermath of the December 2004 Ukrainian presidential elections also yielded a significant joint statement from Russia (albeit reluctantly) and NATO referencing a free and fair electoral process and the rule of law in Ukraine. Secretary of State Powell expressed his encouragement over this joint statement after his December 2004 trip to Brussels when he said he was "pleased that Russia was able to join with NATO in agreeing to the statement." He continued, "I think what we ought to do is accept what we see today in the NATO-Russia Council statement as an expression of the Russian position, and I'm pleased that we leave here today with this union of views with respect to what happens next in Ukraine."[9]

Russia has also been more amenable to cooperation with NATO following the 9/11 attacks and now uses the NRC more and more for this effort. For example, Colonel-General Baluyevsky, chief of the General Staff of the Russian armed forces since June 2004, has met several times with senior NATO personnel. In November 2004 in Mons, Belgium, he met with Gen James Jones, NATO's supreme allied commander. Their consultations centered on expanding the current NATO-Russian military-to-military cooperation plan, which the NRC was discussing. Among the topics covered was the future supply of Russian weapons to the Iraqi army, along with an offer of Russian military training to the new Iraqi army in using these weapons. This is particularly important to Russia, as Iraq has long been a customer of Soviet and Russian weapons systems.[10]

In addition to the NRC, the formal military liaison missions established by both sides have been particularly useful in helping to carry out programs of practical cooperation. Following the installation of a NATO military liaison mission in Moscow in May 2002, NATO and Russia signed additional agreements in April 2004 to create a Russian military liaison office at the NATO Operational Command in Mons and the NATO Transformation Command in Norfolk. The agreements came during NATO secretary general de Hoop Scheffer's visit to Moscow where it was further agreed that the Moscow mission would be strengthened with additional personnel. During his two-day visit, de Hoop Scheffer held talks with President Putin, Foreign Minister Sergei Lavrov, Defense Minister Sergei Ivanov, Secretary of State of the Security Council Igor Ivanov, and members of the Duma. Key issues they discussed included NATO-Russian relations and curbing the proliferation of weapons of mass destruction, among others.[11]

Better Practical Cooperation and Confidence-Building Measures

NATO-Russian military-to-military cooperation had noticeably blossomed by the last quarter of 2003. That year 68 events were scheduled in the areas of interoperability communications events; NATO Defense College events; and other events such as theater missile defense, procedural exercises, defense reform and industries, NRC meetings, transport aircraft and the Cooperative Airspace Agreement, nonlethal weapons, and secure communications. All but three of the 68 events took place with almost 450 Russian and NATO military and civilian officials interacting. More than 186 events were planned through the fall of 2004 in the same general categories, and that number was still rising toward the end of the year. More significantly, approximately 800 Russian and NATO officials were scheduled to work together in these events.[12]

In other practical terms, NATO and Russian foreign ministers at the Istanbul Summit in June 2004 reaffirmed their commitment to continue the military-to-military cooperation the two sides had increased during the previous two years. They also reiterated their adherence to the goals, principles, and commitments contained in the Founding Act, the Rome Declaration, and past NRC decisions, and their determination to stand together against shared threats. They expressed their mutual desire to broaden NRC political dialogue and to promote common approaches and possible future joint actions. They welcomed the concrete, practical contributions the NRC made to Euro-Atlantic security, specifically noting

- their solidarity in their stand against terrorism,

- the success of the March 2004 Theater Missile Defense Command Post Exercise in Colorado,

- the results of the civil emergency planning and response exercise Kaliningrad 2004 hosted by Russia,

- the progress achieved in enhancing military-to-military cooperation and the interoperability of NATO and Russian forces,

- the anticipated completion of the NRC Cooperative Airspace Initiative Feasibility Study by the end of 2004,

- the ongoing work of the NATO-Russian nuclear experts' consultations and the Russian offer to attend a field demonstration on nuclear weapons incident response procedures,

- the Ad Hoc Working Group on Defense Reform to continue ongoing work on interoperability and ongoing efforts to enhance practical work on military-technical cooperation, and

- their resolve to strengthen cooperation in crisis management.

Finally, the ministers again welcomed Russia's offer to provide practical support to the NATO-led International Security Assistance Force (ISAF) in Afghanistan and reaffirmed their commitment to further practical cooperation in this regard.[13]

Russia also agreed in Istanbul to join Operation Active Endeavor, NATO's antiterrorist naval operation in the Mediterranean Sea begun in October 2001.[14] Russia followed up by formally signing an agreement during a December 2004 meeting of the NRC in Brussels. Although NATO and Russian forces have worked together in the Balkans, this operation is significant in that it is carried out under Article 5 of the Washington Treaty and therefore is a formal NATO collective-defense operation. It is noteworthy that plans call for the Russian forces, following training and certification, to operate under NATO command. There will also be a certification process for two Russian ships to participate. This is the first time for Russia to contribute to such a NATO operation.[15]

The Russian navy took part in 10 exercises in 2004—three in the North Atlantic, three in the Baltic, and four in the Mediterranean. A Russian Northern Fleet nuclear submarine also made a port visit to the French port of Brest in a historic, though largely symbolic, event. However, General Baluyevsky indicated the visit signaled a genuine intent to develop further the levels of military cooperation with the alliance, stating, "I am certain that today there are objective conditions to allow Russia to fine-tune a new mode of coordination with NATO."[16]

In addition to the areas mentioned above, the NATO-Russian partnership has had successes in joint intelligence assessments on terrorist threats, future NATO-Russian peacekeeping operations, emergency response exercises in Russia in conjunction with the US Federal Emergency Management Agency (FEMA), and submarine crew escape and rescue. Further highlights include a successful NATO-Russian retraining center for military personnel leaving the Russian armed forces and reintegrating into Russian civilian society, a Russian aircrew survival training program, and experts nearing agreement on a comprehensive common assessment of proliferation dangers.[17]

NATO-Russian operational cooperation continues to grow and strengthen as well. For example, Russia has offered to support the NATO mission in Afghanistan—the International Security Assistance Force—with overflights, transit, and airlift; NATO is now seriously studying this offer.[18] Other programs such as the Cooperative Airspace Agreement and the Airlift Implementing Agreement also were on track for implementation.

Finally, ongoing NATO operations in the Balkans following the allied intervention in Bosnia and Herzegovina provided a good proving ground for burgeoning joint operations with Russia, along with other non-NATO countries. Russian and NATO soldiers have generally worked together effectively since 1996, both within the Implementation Force and later the Stabilization Force in Bosnia and Herzegovina, reflecting the shared goals and joint political responsibility for the implementation of the 1995 Dayton Peace Accords. Although both sides had significant political disagreements over NATO actions in Kosovo during the subsequent low point in their relations, Russia eventually played a vital diplomatic role in securing an end to that conflict. This came about after Russia signed an agreement with NATO in Helsinki following the conclusion of the Military Technical Agreement between NATO and Yugoslav military commanders in June 1999 and the UN Security Council Resolution 1244 of that same month, which established the basis for an international security presence in Kosovo.[19] While this type of cooperation between West and East was certainly unprecedented, it showed the potential for how the two sides could work together, especially in the field. Although NATO and Russian leaders did not always agree on issues, in the field their commanders and forces achieved a remarkable level of cooperation, especially considering their recent past as adversaries.[20]

Cooperation on Russian Defense Reform

Reform of the Russian armed forces is a high priority for both the Russian Federation and NATO and is one of the highest priorities of the NRC. Russia believes the NRC Ad Hoc Working

Group on Defense Reform, set up at the end of 2002, is doing a good job of coordinating cooperation in this area and that the cooperation program is being implemented according to schedule. The expert working groups on manning in the armed forces and on macroeconomic and social aspects of military reform also received high praise from Russian leaders, and two Russian military researchers even began working in September 2004 at the NATO Defense College in Rome.[21]

The need for defense reform in Russia has recently been highlighted in several areas. One of the most problematic is the status of thousands of people who possess unique, potentially dangerous knowledge and skills. Should these skills and knowledge spread uncontrolled, the security of many countries around the world could be jeopardized. Additionally, the Russian defense industry, a major contributor to the Russian economy and GDP (gross domestic product), is in desperate condition. As of 2004, defense-related enterprises are on average operated at less than 22 percent capacity. The physical depreciation of fixed assets is 50 percent, and that of machinery and equipment is up to 70 percent. Furthermore, as much as 95 percent of this machinery and equipment has not been renovated for a decade.[22]

The July 2004 sacking of Gen Anatoly Kvashnin, the controversial and pugnacious chief of the General Staff of the Russian armed forces, and his replacement by Colonel-General Baluyevsky also appear to have helped Russian military cooperation with NATO. Baluyevsky has widespread support throughout Moscow, will work more closely with the civilianized Ministry of Defense, and is considered by many to be one of the finest Russian generals on the General Staff. He has already appeared much more likely to pursue serious military reform than his predecessor, who instead actively pursued only his personal ambitions. Baluyevsky has played a significant part in arms reduction negotiations and was also involved in setting up the NRC.[23] Although Russia has no real national military strategy yet, and no real consensus on one, there is at least now some hope that situation will improve under the leadership of Colonel-General Baluyevsky.

Notes

1. Putin, "Putin Determined to Argue with Bush." Just prior to his February 2005 summit with President Bush in Bratislava, Slovakia, Putin once again emphasized that Russia would not join NATO, as this would mean a partial loss of Russian national sovereignty and certain restrictions in political decision making.

2. Totskiy, "Interview."

3. Rogov, "Window of Opportunity," 72.

4. Rice, "U.S., Europe Looking Beyond."

5. Burns, "NATO and the Transatlantic Relation."

6. Burns, "NATO-Russia Council."

7. Ibid.

8. Totskiy, "Interview."

9. Powell, "Powell Sees Bright Future."

10. McDermott, "General Baluyevsky Building Trust."

11. de Hoop Scheffer, "NATO and Russia Enhance Military."

12. Briefing, NATO Military Liaison.

13. "Chairman's Statement of the Meeting," 90–91.

14. "NATO, Russia Review Cooperative Activities," *United States Mission to NATO.*

15. "Russia to Support NATO's Anti-Terror Effort."

16. McDermott, "General Baluyevsky Building Trust."

17. Fritch, "NATO's Strategic Partnerships."

18. Burns, "NATO-Russia Council."

19. "New Relationships," 39.

20. Kaplan, "NATO's First Fifty Years," 17–19.

21. Totskiy, "Interview."

22. Rubanov, "On the Cooperation with NATO," 68.

23. McDermott, "Baluyevsky."

Chapter 6

Recommendations—The Way Ahead

And above all, don't tell us what to do.

—Mikhail S. Gorbachev

Underlying Issues

In light of the previously mentioned underlying issues that have either caused contention or contributed to better cooperation between NATO and Russia, NATO can and should take a number of recommended actions and policies to foster better relations with Russia. Although there will always be disagreements and contentious issues between NATO and Russia, these recommendations are based on actions that will minimize those contentious issues in the future, along with accentuating the policies that are more likely to contribute to continuing success between the two. This chapter examines specific underlying Russian causes for concern and then describes concrete actions the alliance can take to work together more productively with its Russian partner.

Fear of Encirclement and Need for Security

Throughout the past several centuries, Russians have feared threats to their borders and security from outside powers and forces. Sometimes these fears have been well-founded and sometimes not. However, the Russian perception is that there is always that danger and possibility and that they have to be constantly on guard to do whatever is necessary to prevent it. This is one of the main reasons NATO expansion is such a perceived threat to Russia. After several centuries of invasions from the west (from the Poles, French, and Germans—all of whom are now NATO allies) as well as from the east and south (e.g., the Mongol hordes and the Cossacks), Russians are understandably sensitive to that possibility and very often see Western actions from that viewpoint. As a result, NATO expansion has in many ways alarmed Russians, leading many there to believe NATO's designs on Central and Eastern Europe are to weaken Russia and surround it with the Western alliance.

Russian leaders have also voiced concerns that enlargement would only serve to marginalize Russia, hamper and undermine its efforts to reform, and create unnecessary new divisions throughout Europe. They insisted NATO's eastward expansion would not actually deal effectively with the real security issues facing Europe, but would rather force Russia to react to NATO's moves and would undermine, rather than enhance, European security.[1] Therefore, NATO must proceed carefully in considering its future enlargement. It is clear that the alliance plans to continue its expansion and has left the door open to any country willing and able to meet its entrance requirements. However, as NATO's borders draw closer to Russia's, NATO leaders can expect Russian protests to grow stronger and more resistant.

Some potential NATO members will not raise strong protests from Moscow due to their distance from Russia's borders or clear lack of strong military capability (e.g., Albania or Croatia). However, vehement protests undoubtedly will arise when countries belonging to the Commonwealth of Independent States or directly bordering Russia join NATO, such as Georgia and especially Ukraine, due to its very strong historical, cultural, and economic ties to Russia. If the alliance eventually accepts Ukraine, NATO leaders will have to deal with how to keep Russia on their side and proactively engaged with the alliance without feeling threatened by the presence of the Western alliance on its immediate southwestern flank. NATO must think not only twice, but three times, before finally extending membership to Ukraine and should have a clear understanding of the benefits and drawbacks to this relationship for all parties involved. NATO leaders must also keep in mind Ukraine's necessity to maintain its relationship with Russia and act accordingly.

Alliance leaders also should turn to new NATO members to gain an even better understanding of Russia. The 10 most recent adherents all came out of the shadow and domination of the former Soviet Union and can give the alliance a unique perspective on not only their historic relationship with Moscow, but also the Kremlin's general views and thoughts. To date this perspective has not yet been significantly aired in Brussels. Tomáš Valášek, director of the Brussels office of the Center for Defense Information, asserts this more finely tuned Russian "radar" could definitely benefit NATO, since it would bring to light the knowledge and experience of some of those countries that know Moscow best. NATO's challenge will be to allay any of the irrational fears of these newer members, while tapping into the energy and focus they offer. This is all the more important due to the attention Russia has given to NATO enlargement.[2]

Russia still tends to see current global relationships in more of a nineteenth century "great power" context and mirror that view onto the West, particularly the United States. Russian leaders automatically assume that a great power and geopolitical framework drive Western policy, so they see the net of Western relationships in Eurasia as a form of neo-containment meant to restrict Russian power and influence. It will be vitally important for NATO to continue to pursue economic trade, investment, and engagement, while holding firm to principled policies upholding international law, respect for sovereignty, democracy, and human rights. As Celeste Wallander, director of the Russia and Eurasia Program at the Center for Strategic and International Studies, recently testified at a House hearing on US-Russian relations, "Like the Europeans, the United States needs to more consistently see Russia as a work in progress in which we continue to have a very large stake."[3] NATO must also continue to see the very large stake it has in Russia's success and security.

One insight into how to proceed may come from the Russian perspective itself. Russia has been clear and firm regarding its own prospects of future membership in NATO. President Putin has said many times that Russia has no aspirations to join NATO. General Totskiy explained further that the issue of membership is not especially relevant to Moscow.

> What is more important is the way in which relations between nations, or alliances of nations, are built, and on what basis; the aims they pursue in their cooperation; and the benefit this cooperation brings to others. We believe that NATO-Russia relations form a natural part of Europe's evolving security architecture and that the NRC is becoming a pillar of international relations. NATO and Russia have taken on a serious commitment for the future of Europe. And as far as this Mission is

concerned, it makes no difference whether we join the Alliance or cooperate on a different basis.[4]

NATO leaders must, above all else, ensure that Russia continues to understand that NATO has and will always have a serious commitment to Russia for the future security of Europe.

The key for NATO leaders during any future expansion will be to ensure that Russia still believes it is in Europe's overall best interest for more countries, such as Ukraine, to join NATO—a tall order indeed. While doing this, they must also keep uppermost in mind the inescapable fact that geography matters to Russia and must continue to find ways to make the benefits to Russia of NATO expansion outweigh the perceived losses of geographic security. This also applies to NATO's future deployments of troops on the soil of new members from Central and Eastern Europe. The purpose of these deployments must be clearly portrayed to Russia, and more importantly *understood by them*, as not posing any threat to Russian security. NATO must continue to engage and include Russia in the planning and execution of alliance exercises and even operations, so that Russian leaders understand the value NATO leaders place on their participation, while at the same time encouraging Russian responsibility and active participation.

The Need to Be Respected

Another critical component to the Russian mind is the need to be respected by the world. More than almost anything, Russia wants to be respected and treated as an equal to other countries and to be considered the great power Russians feel she is. In a revealing episode in 1992, shortly after the dissolution of the Soviet Union, Ambassador Catto, then head of the US Information Agency (USIA), had the opportunity to interview former Soviet president Mikhail Gorbachev. Gorbachev passed on a message through Ambassador Catto for US decision makers that still applies today: "Make up your mind what you want Russia to be. Is she a great power to be worked with or a candidate for breaking into even smaller pieces? And above all, don't tell us what to do."[5]

Following the dissolution of the Soviet Union and the ensuing challenges to its economy and society, Russians have struggled to regain not only the foundations of their society and national strength, but also the respect of the world they feel they have lost over the past 15 years. The author saw firsthand this desire for respect during one of the many Russian delegations he took to the United States during his time at the US Embassy in Moscow. During this trip, the delegation visited Fort Carson in Colorado Springs, Colorado, and toured the state-of-the-art tank simulators at the base. The author was quite impressed—even as a US military officer accustomed to high-tech equipment—and later asked some of the delegation members for their impressions. "*Normal'no* (normal)," they casually shrugged, as if to say it was exactly like what they have in Russia. However, having lived and worked in Russia, the author knew far better. But it was clear they wanted very much to be respected and to have other countries not think poorly of them or of their capabilities.

At a recent US House of Representatives hearing on developments in US-Russian relations, Cong. Curt Weldon gave a summary of how the West should treat Russia. In his testimony, he asserted that "they don't want our money—they want our respect! If we are going to call them partners, we need to treat them like partners. For us to have the respect of Russia, we have to give them our respect."[6] To Russians, this means listening to them, not "telling them what to do," and not prying into their internal affairs. On this latter issue, NATO will have to continue to walk its tightrope of insisting on conformity to international law and norms of behavior, especially in areas such as Chechnya, while at the same time not being seen as meddling in the otherwise legitimate internal politics of a sovereign nation.

Desire for Economic Prosperity

One of the strongest driving forces in Russian foreign and economic policy is its desperate need to rebuild its economic foundation. Russia's foreign policy is greatly influenced by its economic interests for the sake of power, autonomy, and global position. Although economic interests do not solely drive Russian foreign policy, they are extremely important to it.[7] NATO should continue to find a way to engage Russia economically, realizing the current limitations to Russia's finances. Economic incentives go far in this regard, and NATO must find ways to continue to develop trade with Russia, perhaps through its energy sector or even through its military-industrial complex and arms capabilities.

Russia has made clear its desire to join the World Trade Organization, a move that would be in NATO's best interest, provided Russia can meet the entry requirements. The United States supports this endeavor. President Bush reaffirmed this when he and President Putin held a joint press conference in Bratislava after their February 2005 summit, saying the two leaders had "agreed to accelerate negotiations for Russia's entry into the WTO."[8] It is also worth noting that President Putin made a special effort to thank President Bush for the "serious message" that Russian negotiators noticed in the course of the WTO negotiations during the summit. Putin said it was "a message aimed at resolving all the problems that stand in the way of Russia's accession to the WTO" and opined that "not only the Russian economy, but also the US economy are interested in the positive outcome."[9]

Leading intelligence experts also highlight the importance of a strong Russian economy to the security of Europe and of the role Europe can play in drawing Russia closer. In their view, if Russia knows Western Europe wants to forge a "special relationship" with a Russia that is economically stronger, Moscow is more likely to be tolerant of former Soviet states moving closer to Europe.[10] Such a closer relationship to European institutions and structures would also provide Russia a vital counterweight to the strong economic lure of weapons of mass destruction and other weapons proliferation, as well as reducing its perceived need for growing ties with other regions and countries, such as China, India, and Iran. President Putin has made clear this Russian need and desire for further development, stating shortly after his reelection in March 2004,

> the main goal of our policy is not to demonstrate some or other imperial ambitions, but rather to secure favorable external conditions for the development of Russia. There is nothing unusual in that. And we will be building a multi-vector foreign policy; we will work together with the United States, the European Union, and with individual countries of Europe. We will work together with our Asian partners, with China, India, and with countries of the Asia-Pacific region.[11]

As a result, the support of NATO and other Western institutions takes on vital importance in keeping Russia positively engaged in and cooperating with the rest of Europe.

Need for a Strong Euro-Atlantic Security Framework and Dialogue

Russia is now more readily acknowledging, at least publicly, the value of NATO and of closer relations with the alliance. Amb. Anatoly Adamishin, president of the Russian Association for Euro-Atlantic Cooperation, recently affirmed this view when he opined that NATO-Russian relations are currently exemplary, despite some disagreements. As he pointed out, Russia must "have an alliance with the Alliance," and any quarrels between the two must be settled without taking sides. He put it plainly when he said, "NATO is necessary." The challenge, he said, is to avoid tackling new problems with old, obsolete methods.[12]

It is vital for the alliance to encourage this view and to keep Russia engaged with the West. Without a continuation of strong, active, and regular engagement from NATO and other important Western institutions (e.g., the EU), Russia naturally will look for support, security, and prosperity from other sources (e.g., China, India, and even Iran) if they offer much-needed economic capital for Russia. NATO's European members will be particularly key players in this regard, both multilaterally and even bilaterally, as Moscow looks more and more toward integration into European institutions and seeks to regain what it considers its rightful, prominent role on the continent.

Without such continued active engagement, NATO could face a hardening of Russian attitudes toward the West. The likely result would be for Russia to close more of its society and become even more secretive than it already is, clearly a step backward from the alliance's goal of transparency. NATO has to avoid these pitfalls, insofar as it can possibly influence them. Above all, NATO should avoid marginalizing Russia, which will take creativity as NATO's borders expand further eastward. The alliance could encourage a more active Russian role in the PfP, include more Russian officers in technical ventures such as joint exercises and force planning, and even possibly integrate Russia into its own efforts at military reform.[13] One thing NATO

45

leaders can count on is that as NATO expands its membership, especially to the east, Russia will continue to look more to other nations to establish or strengthen other alliances and partnerships in response.

NATO's leaders also must keep in mind that words matter to the Russians. The details and exact wording of international treaties, agreements, and even simple diplomatic notes matter. The author saw this repeatedly during his time in Moscow, when reaching agreement on the seemingly smallest details sometimes took excruciating lengths of time. In the Russian view, the spirit and intent of an agreement cannot necessarily be proven—only that which is written can be proven. Accurate words also prevent a subsequent administration or government from changing the intent of an agreement without resorting to formal channels. Russian leaders believe they can avoid being cheated or taken advantage of by correctly spelling out everything. Conversely, they do not see a problem in taking advantage of loopholes in treaties and agreements, if the *letter* of the law is not violated. In their view, it is perfectly fair, even if it might violate the *intent* of the law. Otherwise, their treaty partner should have seen this possibility and guarded against it. The moral: Whenever alliance leaders can join formally with Russia in an activity or partnership, they should do it.

Close, honest, and transparent dialogue is critical to NATO success in continuing to engage Russia, and the NRC definitely has been a step in the right direction. Fortunately, the alliance has recognized this and should do everything it possibly can to encourage dialogue. Amb. Maurizio Moreno, Italian permanent representative to the North Atlantic Council, recently commented on the importance of dialogue regarding NATO's new history in its relations with Russia. In his view, Russia is now an equal partner, and the process within the NRC is working well, even on sensitive issues such as Iraq, Afghanistan, Georgia, and the controversial Ukrainian presidential election. Although there are natural differences of opinions, and even some differences between NATO and Russian values, he believes the two sides can work successfully through these challenges. According to Moreno, "There *are* values we can share," and he stated that we have done so recently through the NRC. Although Russia has not joined NATO, and most likely will not, in his view there is still the definite possibility for beneficial and productive dialogue.[14]

Former NATO secretary general Lord Robertson captured the essence of NATO's success in the NRC when he presciently stated in 2002, "The real difference between '19 + 1' and '20' is not a question of mathematics, but one of chemistry: the success of the NATO-Russia Council will depend on the political will of the participants." Based on the apparent willingness of both sides to make it work, he believed that "the prospects for a genuinely new quality in NATO-Russia relations appear bright."[15]

Thus far, his belief in the NRC's prospects has proven well founded. Now, it is up to NATO and Russian leaders to ensure that the chemistry remains strong and positive. This will undoubtedly require a skillful mix of patient dialogue combined at times with more forceful pressure, without resorting to confrontation. As history has shown, confrontation, demands, and ultimatums will accomplish very little with Russia (as indeed, these tactics accomplish little with any country). The best prospects for NATO-Russian relations will result from NATO leaders honestly listening to and considering Russian views, even if in the end Moscow does not like the answer. To the extent possible, NATO must avoid marginalizing Russia.

Need for Conflict Resolution, Crisis Management, and Greater Interoperability

In today's challenging world security environment, it is more important than ever that NATO and Russia find ways to cooperate effectively in conflict resolution, peacekeeping, and crisis-management operations. Much is already being done, and NATO leaders should continue this positive trend toward greater cooperation and interoperability of NATO and Russian armed forces. For example, NATO and Russia are preparing the groundwork for cooperation in peacekeeping in several areas for possible future joint operations. The NRC Working Group on Peacekeeping has prepared a joint document titled "Political Aspects of the Generic Concept of NATO-Russia Joint Peacekeeping Operations," which is being tested in procedural exercises. In addition, a program for improving interoperability between NATO and Russian peacekeeping units has been approved and is being implemented.[16]

In considering whether Russia would join NATO in crisis-management operations, the Russian view is that the United Nations should play the lead role. This view is understandable, since Russia is a permanent member of the UN Security Council and holds veto power. Still, Russia recently has shown much more willingness to operate together with the alliance and has agreed to help out in current hot spots such as Afghanistan and Iraq to a limited extent. As to whether Russia is prepared in principle to conduct further joint operations with NATO—even outside NATO's traditional area of responsibility, as it already has done in Afghanistan and the Balkans—Russian leaders don't "rule out this possibility."[17]

A useful example of good cooperation, for the most part, is the joint operations NATO and Russian forces have conducted in Bosnia and Herzegovina. In the Balkans, NATO and Russian forces showed that they have the capability to work together effectively, given the right circumstances and the will to succeed. From the Russian viewpoint, when joint forces have clear tasking and are working under a UN Security Council mandate, they are perfectly capable of operating effectively together in the most difficult conditions. General Totskiy proudly related that "Russian soldiers and commanders, who worked shoulder to shoulder with their NATO colleagues, have fond memories of the spirit of camaraderie and cooperation, which frequently provided a source of support during the difficult days of the Balkan operations."[18]

Despite goodwill and national resolve, NATO and Russian forces remain a long way apart from anything close to true military interoperability. However, the encouraging cooperation within the NRC also is yielding broader cooperation within the EAPC and the PfP. Both NATO and Russia now have the opportunity to take that cooperation and bring greater technical interoperability to their military forces, communications equipment, aircraft, naval vessels, and other fields. This will require money, something Russia and some NATO member nations lack. However, one productive way to accomplish the goal is through deeper Russian engagement in existing practical cooperative projects in the PfP framework, with the final goal of developing true joint capabilities between both parties' armed forces.[19]

The Bottom Line

Much of the NATO-Russian relationship can be determined by the attitude of cooperation from the alliance. Martin van Heuven, former US deputy permanent representative to the European Office of the UN and International Organizations in Geneva and former member of the US National Intelligence Council, summarized the benefits of this cooperation, pointing out that,

> a purposeful Western policy of cooperation will remain important to help Russia reform and to meet the sensitive issue of Russia's perception of itself as a world power. But Western cooperation will be validated only to the degree reform will create some form of dependency on the West, creating mutual incentives for cooperation. . . . An unstable Russia would make for an unstable Europe. On the other hand, a Russia that is focused forward on reform rather than backward on lost empire, and that cooperates with NATO will be an indispensable and positive factor in European security. This should be the continuing objective of NATO policy.[20]

Western institutions in general and NATO in particular should continue their strong focus on giving Russia a genuine voice in international decision making. Otherwise, Russia will not perceive itself to have the same stake in these institutions as its Western members and will continue to look to other partners, such as China and India, for support and security. Russia will undoubtedly not become a member of all Western institutions, but it can still play a vital role and, more importantly, remain more closely integrated with these institutions. Granted, Russia must still show significant reform in several different areas in order to be taken seriously by Western institutions and integrated more closely into their structures. However, without weakening its own position or influence, the West can also still ensure that Moscow has a legitimate international voice commensurate with its perceived "great power" role, reasonable and competitive economic possibilities compatible with its own goals, and the opportunity to agree on many international foreign policy goals, even if some disagreements still exist over the means to those goals.[21]

In the end, NATO must decide what kind of relationship it can and should have with Russia, keeping the long term in view. NATO should be a constructive partner and be able to understand the complexities of the situation the Kremlin leadership is facing. Alliance leaders should give a clear and consistent message of support and engagement to Russia and should stand firm on those issues that involve its core interests and principles.[22] Above all, NATO must convince Russia that it honestly has Russia's best interests at heart and that Moscow faces no threat from the alliance.

Conclusion

In considering the future of NATO-Russian relations, there are reasons to be hopeful. There have been many accomplishments, and the road ahead, while filled with certain challenges, still looks passable. However, both sides will have to continue their current course of cooperation and keep their focus on the will to work productively together. When the inevitable challenges and disagreements arise, both sides must remain committed to work through them, just as in any successful marriage. The most successful cooperation will undoubtedly arise from a framework of stability, confidence, predictability, and transparency in the NATO-Russian relationship. Such a relationship can lead to even more shared responsibility for joint decision making and consensus building, as well as continuing to encourage a practical agenda for Euro-Atlantic security.[23]

Geopolitics will continue to play a significant role. As mentioned above, Russia straddles two continents—Europe and Asia—and the double-headed eagle on the Russian crest continues to watch over both directions of the empire. NATO's challenge will be to ensure that the western view from the Kremlin looks much closer and reassuring than it has in the past and to ensure that Russia's leaders know without doubt that they are a vital, integral part of the European security structure.

What the future holds for Russian democratic reforms and closer integration into the West remains clouded. Some of the initial steps toward real progress and openness Russia showed over the past 15 years seem to be regressing under various reforms implemented by President Putin. While the final destination of Russia's current path remains unknown, it is certain that, regardless of where it leads, NATO and Russian leaders will have their commitment to the relationship tested again and again. The future of the NATO-Russian relationship hangs predominantly on their will to make it work.

Notes

1. Clark et al., *Permanent Alliance?* 20.
2. Valášek, "The Meaning of Enlargement," 10.
3. House, *Developments in U.S.-Russia Relations.* See testimony of Celeste A. Wallander, 6–7.
4. Totskiy, "Interview."
5. Catto, *Ambassadors at Sea*, 335–36.
6. House, *Developments in U.S.-Russia Relations.* See testimony of Cong. Curt Weldon.
7. Ibid., 4.
8. "Bush, Putin Address Concerns."
9. Ibid.
10. National Intelligence Council, *Mapping the Global Future*, 74.
11. Torkunov, "Russia and the West," 3–4.
12. Adamishin, address.
13. *Twain Shall Meet*, 13.
14. Moreno, address.
15. Robertson, "Introduction," 5.
16. Totskiy, "Interview."
17. Ibid.
18. Ibid.
19. Fritch, "NATO's Strategic Partnerships."
20. van Heuven, *NATO in 2010*, 3, 6.
21. *Twain Shall Meet*, 5.
22. House, *Developments in U.S.-Russia Relations.* See Prepared Statement by Eugene B. Rumer, 4.
23. For a more detailed analysis, see Rogov, "Window of Opportunity."

Bibliography

Adamishin, Anatoly, president of the Russian Association for Euro-Atlantic Cooperation. Address. "New NATO and Its Partnerships." Atlantic Treaty Association 50th General Assembly Convention, Rome, Italy, 1 December 2004.

"Air Policing over the Baltics." *NATO Supreme Headquarters Allied Powers Europe (SHAPE) News*, 31 March 2004. http://www.nato.int/shape/news/2004/03/i040331.htm (accessed 18 November 2004).

"Alliance's Strategic Concept." NATO Press Release, 23 April 1999. http://www.nato.int/docu/pr/1999/p99-065e.htm.

Baluyevsky, Yuri. "General Baluyevsky: Russia Does Not Fear NATO Expansion." *On-Line Pravda*, 27 May 2002. http://english.pravda.ru/politics/2002/05/27/29320.html.

Bennett, Christopher. "Building Effective Partnerships." *NATO Review-Istanbul Summit Special*, June 2004.

Burns, R. Nicholas. "NATO and the Transatlantic Relation." *United States Mission to NATO*, 8 November 2004. http://nato.usmission.gov/ambassador/2004/2004Nov08_Burns_Berlin.htm (accessed 18 November 2004).

———. "NATO-Russia Council: A Vital Partnership in the War on Terror." *United States Mission to NATO*, 4 November 2004. http://nato.usmission.gov/ambassador/2004/2004Nov04_Burns_Moscow.htm (accessed 18 November 2004).

———. "Pre-Ministerial Briefing with Journalists." *United States Mission to NATO*, 6 December 2004. http://nato.usmission.gov/ambassador/2004/2004Dec06_Burns_Brussels.htm.

Bush, George. "President Discusses American and European Alliance in Belgium." *United States Mission to NATO*, 21 February 2005. http://www.whitehouse.gov/news/releases/2005/02/20050221.html.

"Bush, Putin Address Concerns about Russian Democracy." *United States Mission to NATO*, 24 February 2005. http://nato.usmission.gov/Article.asp?ID=235C74C6-32D7-48B7-8667-3AC52F69161C.

Catto, Henry E., Jr. *Ambassadors at Sea: The High and Low Adventures of a Diplomat.* Austin, TX: University of Texas Press, 1998.

Clark, Wesley K., Charles W. Freeman Jr., Max Cleland, and Gordon Smith. *Permanent Alliance? NATO's Prague Summit and Beyond.* Washington, DC: Atlantic Council of the United States, April 2001.

"The Euro-Atlantic Partnership." *NATO Topics*, 31 March 2004. http://www.nato.int/issues/eap/index.html (accessed 7 September 2004).

Fritch, Paul. "NATO's Strategic Partnerships: Building Hope on Experience." *NATO Review*, Autumn 2003. http://www.nato.int/docu/review/2003/issue3/english/art3.html.

Heuven, Martin H. A. van. *NATO in 2020.* Washington, DC: Atlantic Council of the United States, August 1999. http://acus.org/docs/9908-NATO_2010.pdf.

Hoop Scheffer, NATO Secretary General Jaap de. Address. Atlantic Treaty Association 50th General Assembly Convention, Rome, Italy, 1 December 2004.

———. "NATO and Russia Enhance Military Cooperation." *NATO Update*, 7–8 April 2004. http://www.nato.int/docu/update/2004/04-april/e0407c.htm (accessed 16 April 2004).

———. "NATO, Russia Enhance Military Cooperation." *United States Mission to NATO*, 14 April 2004. http://nato.usmission.gov/Article.asp?ID=70E14E9A-4D76-4469-8344-278F2E8D0042 (accessed 15 April 2005).

———. "Opening Remarks." *NATO Speeches—NATO Summit*, 22 February 2005. http://www.nato.int/docu/speech/2005/s050222a.htm.

———. "Opening Statement at the Press Conference Following the Meeting of the NATO-Ukraine Council at the Level of Heads of State and Government." *NATO Speeches—NATO Summit*, 22 February 2005. http://www.nato.int/docu/speech/2005/s050222f.htm.

House. *Developments in U.S.-Russia Relations: Hearing before the Subcommittee on Europe and Emerging Threats of the Committee on International Relations.* 109th Cong., 1st sess., 9 March 2005. http://wwwa.house.gov/international_relation/109/99821.pdf.

Jones, Gen James L., supreme allied commander Europe, NATO. Address. Atlantic Treaty Association 50th General Assembly Convention, Rome, Italy, 1 December 2004.

Kaplan, Lawrence S. *Long Entanglement: NATO's First Fifty Years.* Westport, CT: Praeger, 1999.

Kelin, Andrei. "Attitude to NATO Expansion: Calmly Negative." *International Affairs: A Russian Journal of World Politics, Diplomacy and International Relations* 50, no. 1 (2004): 17–25.

Kuchma, Leonid. "Message from Leonid Kuchma, President of Ukraine." *NATO Review: 50th Anniversary Commemorative Edition,* 1999.

Kuznetsova, Ekaterina. "NATO: New Anti-Terrorist Organization?" *International Affairs: A Russian Journal of World Politics, Diplomacy and International Relations* 50, no. 3 (2004): 22–26.

MacKenzie, David, and Michael W. Curran. *A History of Russia and the Soviet Union.* Rev. ed. Homewood, IL: The Dorsey Press, 1982.

McDermott, Roger. "Baluyevsky: New Chief of the Russian General Staff." *Jamestown Foundation Eurasia Daily Monitor* 1, no. 56, 21 July 2004. http://www.jamestown.org/publications _details.php?volume_id=401&issue_id=3022&article_id =2368275.

———. "General Baluyevsky Building Trust with NATO." *Jamestown Foundation Eurasia Daily Monitor* 1, no. 128, 16 November 2004. http://www.jamestown.org/publications_details .php?volume_id=401&issue_id=3142&article_id=2368858.

Moreno, Maurizio, Italian permanent representative to the North Atlantic Council. Address. Atlantic Treaty Association 50th General Assembly Convention, Rome, Italy, 1 December 2004.

Mroziewicz, Robert. "Enlargement and the Capabilities Gap." In *Transforming NATO Forces: European Perspectives.* Edited by C. Richard Nelson and Jason S. Purcell. Washington, DC: The Atlantic Council of the United States, January 2003.

National Intelligence Council. *Mapping the Global Future: Report of the National Intelligence Council's 2020 Project, Based on Consultations with Nongovernmental Experts around the World.* Washington, DC: Government Printing Office, December 2004.

NATO. "Chairman's Statement: Meeting of the NATO-Russia Council at the level of Foreign Ministers held in Istanbul."

Brussels: NATO Press Release, 28 June 2004. http://www
.nato.int/docu/pr/2004/p040628e.htm.

———. "Further Developing NATO-Ukraine Relations." *NATO-Istanbul Summit Reader's Guide*, 2004, 128–32. http://
www.nato.int/docu/rdr-gde-ist/rdr-gde-ist-e.pdf.

———. "Growing NATO-Russian Cooperation." *NATO-Istanbul Summit Reader's Guide*, 2004, 122–27. http://www.nato.int/
docu/rdr-gde-ist/rdr-gde-ist-e.pdf.

———. "NATO after Istanbul: Expanding Operations, Improving Capabilities, Enhancing Cooperation." NATO On-line Library, 14 July 2004. http://www.nato.int/docu/nato
_after_istanbul/nato_after_instanbul_en.pdf (accessed 7 September 2004).

———. "NATO in the 21st Century." Brussels: NATO On-line Library, 13 April 2005. http://www.nato.int/docu/21-cent/
html_en/21st01.html.

———. "NATO Lauded as 'Centerpiece' of U.S. Efforts in Europe." *United States Mission to NATO*, 21 February 2005. http://
nato.usmission.gov/Article.asp?ID=7A10F6CE-5894-431
E-9372-B38896E62FEA.

———. *NATO-Russia: Forging Deeper Relations.* Brussels: NATO Public Diplomacy Division, 2004.

———. "NATO-Russia Council." *NATO Issues*, 30 August 2004. http://www.nato.int/issues/nrc/index.html (accessed 7 September 2004).

———. "NATO-Russia Relations." *NATO Issues*, 30 August 2004. http://www.nato.int/issues/nato-russia/index.html (accessed 7 September 2004).

———. "NATO-Russia Relations: A New Quality. Declaration by Heads of State and Government of NATO Member States and the Russian Federation." *NATO-Russia Council: Rome Summit 2002.* Brussels: NATO Office of Information and Press, 2002.

———. "NATO, Russia Review Cooperative Activities." *United States Mission to NATO*, 28 June 2004. http://nato.us
mission.gov/Article.asp?ID=783FB225-A31D-4CB4-9EA
4-01277CB9DE25.

———. *NATO Transformed.* Brussels: NATO On-line Library, June 2004. http://www.nato.int/docu/nato-trans/html_en/
nato_trans01.html.

———. "NATO-Ukraine: A Distinctive Partnership." Brussels: NATO On-line Library, June 2004. http://www.nato.int/docu/nato-ukraine/html_en/nato_ukraine01.html.

———. "New Relationships: Practical Cooperation and Dialogue." *The Prague Summit and NATO's Transformation: A Reader's Guide.* Brussels: NATO Public Diplomacy Division, 2003.

"NATO Envoy to Visit Georgia." *Online Magazine–Civil Georgia*, 1 February 2005. http://www.una.org.ge/publicat.html.

Powell, Colin. "Powell Sees Bright Future for NATO." *United States Mission to NATO*, 9 December 2004. http://www.state.gov/secretary/former/powell/remarks/39635.htm.

———. "Russia Need Not Worry over NATO Enlargement, Powell Says." *United States Mission to NATO*, 4 April 2004. http://nato.usmission.gov/Article.asp?ID=86EB170C-9938-4898-B7C5-4D5A0E98289A (accessed 13 September 2004).

Putin, Vladimir. Address. *NATO-Russia Council: Rome Summit 2002.* Brussels: NATO Office of Information and Press, 2002.

———. "Putin Determined to Argue with Bush during Russia-USA Summit in Bratislava." *On-Line Pravda*, 24 February 2005. http://english.pravda.ru/main/18/88/354/15010_summit.html.

Rice, Condoleezza. "Remarks at the North Atlantic Treaty Organization Headquarters." *U.S. Department of State*, 9 February 2005. http://www.state.gov/secretary/rm/2005/42047.htm.

———. "U.S., Europe Looking Beyond Past Disagreements, Rice Says." *United States Mission to NATO*, 10 February 2005. http://nato.usmission.gov/Article.asp?ID=C3C71785-2D58-4F74-952D-AFF87A086846.htm.

Robertson, Lord George. "Introduction." In *NATO-Russia Council: Rome Summit 2002.* Brussels: NATO Office of Information and Press, 2002.

Rogov, Sergey. "The Window of Opportunity in Russian-Western Relations." In *The Twain Shall Meet: The Prospects for Russia-West Relations.* Washington, DC: Atlantic Council of the United States, September 2002.

Rubanov, Vladimir. "On the Cooperation with NATO in Defense Industry." In *International Affairs: A Russian Journal of World Politics, Diplomacy and International Relations* 50, no. 6 (2004): 68–78.

"Russia to Support NATO's Anti-Terror Effort in Mediterranean." *United States Mission to NATO*, 10 December 2004. http://nato.usmission.gov/Article.asp?ID=6F07739A-AE 27-47D8-AB7E-3A6D604FB7B8.

Stanhope, Adm Sir Mark, deputy supreme allied commander Transformation (DSACT), NATO. Address. Atlantic Treaty Association 50th General Assembly Convention, Rome, Italy, 1 December 2004.

"Statement Issued by the Heads of State and Government participating in a meeting of the North Atlantic Council in Brussels." *NATO On-Line Library: NATO Press Release*, 22 February 2005. http://www.nato.int/docu/pr/2005/ p05-022e.htm.

Torkunov, Anatolii. "Russia and the West: Common Security Interests." *International Affairs: A Russian Journal of World Politics, Diplomacy and International Relations* 50, no. 4 (2004): 1–6.

Totskiy, Konstantin V. "Interview—General Totskiy: Russian Ambassador to NATO." *NATO Review*, Autumn 2003. http://www.nato.int/docu/review/2003/issue3/english/ art3.html.

Troitski, Mikhail. *Transatlantic Union 1991–2004: Transformation of the U.S.-European Partnership in the Post-Bipolar World* (in Russian). Moscow: Institute for the U.S. and Canadian Studies, Russian Academy of Sciences, 2004.

Valášek, Tomáš. "Meaning of Enlargement." *NATO Review-Istanbul Summit Special*, June 2004.

Vershbow, Alexander. "United States and Russia: The Next Four Years." Remarks at the Woodrow Wilson School of Public and International Affairs at Princeton University. In "Vershbow Sees 'Strong, Positive' U.S. Relationship with Russia." *United States Mission to NATO*, 17 November 2004. http://nato.usmission.gov/Article.asp?ID=786EAE89 -D432-4795-93EA-E0F33FA782C9 (accessed 18 November 2004).

"Vote in Parliament Raises Stakes in Row With Moscow." *Washington Post Metro Express*, 11 March 2005.

Welberts, Rolf. "Explaining NATO in Russia." *NATO Review*, Autumn 2003. http://www.nato.int/docu/review/2003/ issue3/english/art3.html.

Yuryev, Col-Gen Yevgeniy. "Kant Air Base: The First Year Has Passed." *Moscow Krasnaya Zvezda in Russian*, 22 October 2004. http://www.redstar.ru/2004/10/22_10/index.shtml.

Yushchenko, Viktor. "Opening Statement at the Meeting of the NATO-Ukraine Council at the Level of Heads of State and Government." *NATO Speeches—NATO Summit*, 22 February 2005. http://www.nato.int/docu/speech/2005/s050222e .htm.

———. "Opening Statement at the Press Conference following the Meeting of the NATO-Ukraine Council at the Level of Heads of State and Government." *NATO Speeches—NATO Summit*, 22 February 2005. http://www.nato.int/docu/ speech/2005/s050222g.htm.

The Future of NATO-Russian Relations

or How to Dance with a Bear and Not Get Mauled

Air University Press Team

Chief Editor
Jerry L. Gantt

Copy Editor
Sherry C. Terrell

Book Design and Cover Art
Steven C. Garst

Composition and Prepress Production
Ann Bailey

Quality Review
Mary J. Moore

Print Preparation
Joan Hickey

Distribution
Diane Clark